Stepping Out Of The Bubble:

Reflections on the Pilgrimage of Counseling Therapy

Stepping Out Of The Bubble:

Reflections on the Pilgrimage of Counseling Therapy

James P. Krehbiel, Ed. S., LPC, CCBT

About The Author

James P. Krehbiel, Ed.S., LPC, CCBT received his counseling training at Northern Illinois University. James is a Licensed Professional Counselor and Nationally Certified Cognitive-Behavioral Therapist. He currently works as a private practice counselor in Scottsdale, Arizona. He employs a cognitive-behavioral approach in dealing with patients with anxiety and depressive disorders. James has worked in the field of education, including counselor education and therapy. He worked as a teacher and guidance counselor in schools in Illinois and Arizona and has taught graduate-level counselor education courses for Chapman University of California. In 1999, he received the Educator of the Year Award from the Sun Lakes Rotary for his contribution to the Chandler, Arizona School District. He is an active member of the American Mental Health Counselors Association and the National Association of Cognitive-Behavioral Therapists. James has written extensively on topics related to children, families, and couples. His most recent articles include *Talk Therapy's Response to Pain Management,* and *Eating Disorders: Two Sides of the Same Coin.* James is married and has four children and three grandchildren.

Acknowledgments

This work expresses my experience into the journey of psychotherapy. It has always been my desire that the lives of the people I work with will be better off for my entrance into their struggles and the process of healing. There are many people who have assisted me in the development of this book. I cannot personally thank all of them for their contribution. Special credit, however, is deserving of those who encouraged me along the way: My psychiatrist friend and colleague, Nasser Djavadi, M.D., who provided me with much needed support. I would like to thank Barbara Myrick, Eileen Stephens, and Ray Husband who have been mentors and supportive associates of mine. Also, I would like to acknowledge and thank Fred Hanna, Ph.D. of Johns Hopkins University who was a significant influence in my counseling education training at Northern Illinois University. I would like to express appreciation for the writings of M. Scott Peck which served as an inspiration for the foundation of this work. Most importantly, I owe a debt of gratitude to my dear wife, Andrea for assisting me in my writing and being there for me through every step of this process.

Table of Contents

INTRODUCTION

I recall seeing a movie years ago entitled, *The Boy in the Plastic Bubble.* It was produced in the 1970's and was based on a true story about a child. John Travolta played the part of a child who had an immune deficiency disorder from birth, which kept him insulated from the outside world. He was forced to live inside an oxygen-filled bubble that was free of all contaminants. This youngster's life was highly restricted in spite of all the efforts by doctors and his parents. He was very dependent upon his parents for everything in his life, as well as all of his basic needs. This bright and insightful child experienced all the normal emotions that one would display in feeling trapped within the confines of a contaminant free bubble. Many times his emotional outbursts would indicate the degree of his unhappiness. During adolescence he became more frustrated about the confined nature of his life. Although he eventually was able to use a space suit for increased mobility, it was awkward and confining. During adolescence he was restricted from experiencing the fullness of life, free of the bondage of his bubble. He missed the joy of activities that typical kids his age enjoyed. Eventually he fell in love with a girl who was his next-door neighbor. She would come and visit him and she introduced him to her other friends. Desperately, he longed to be out of confinement and experience the fullness of a relationship with his female friend. He finally decided that he had to make a choice to live in confinement for the remainder of his life, or to risk loving which came with stepping out of the bubble. Without hesitation, he made a choice without the knowledge and approval of his parents and doctor. He decided to leave the restrictiveness of the bubble.

This young man was well aware of the possible consequences of his choice, but moved in the direction of his choosing anyway. He knew that contaminants in the air could kill him, but he ignored the warnings. What was it that made him take that kind of a risk? It obviously wasn't a reasonable choice considering the consequences. He made the choice because living life to the fullest at that moment was more important than the implications of continuing to live a restricted life. One day, one month, one year of feeling alive was more important than the risks associated with his choice. He wanted to feel, touch, and experience the activities that most kids his age were able to enjoy. He thought about it, and chose without regret.

Most choices that we make in our lives are not as dramatic as the "boy in the bubble." Yet many of us feel encapsulated due to avoiding choices that potentially would create meaning in our lives. We perpetually avoid purposeful and meaningful decisions that may enrich our experience. Although we may feel restricted or trapped, we may resist opportunities to change behaviors that can lead us toward spiritual and psychological growth.

The purpose of this book is to assist the reader in moving toward a more conscious, adaptive manner of coping with the reality of everyday problems and challenges. It has been my experience personally and through my clinical practice that most individuals are searching for a clearer sense of direction for their lives. They may realize that something is amiss, but are unable to recognize the full scope of their problems. Even after identifying issues, many of us spend a great deal of time and energy resisting a path that will lead us to adopt more enriching patterns of living.

Often, moving a client toward more responsible, fulfilling behavior means becoming aware of the "dusty corners" of one's personality. Since self-discovery can be a painful process, many clients would prefer to avoid it. The question to my clients is, "Do you want to stay in an impasse, or do you want to meet the challenges which arise out of the prospect of behavioral change?" Since change is scary, one must choose. "Do I stay in the comfort zone which may represent archaic and self-defeating patterns of thinking and behaving, or do I "stick my neck out" and create some upheaval that will ultimately lead to a new and more meaningful lifestyle?" Choosing to change one's behavior requires courage and the will to act. The process is not easy, but it can be rewarding. If one can grasp the meaning behind living in the moment, then it becomes easier to move forward and experience the legitimate suffering necessary to get to the growth zone. I hope that this book inspires my readers to live life with more awareness, authenticity, courage and meaning.

I. REFLECTIONS ON LEAVING THE BUBBLE

Although we may not have an immune deficiency disorder which is life threatening, most of us know what it's like to feel encapsulated. We know what it's like to feel powerless, helpless and trapped. We feel like life is passing us by without being a participant. We feel underutilized and live on the perimeter of experience. Being in the bubble may make us feel secure, but at the same time we may feel a calling to move out of the comfort zone. Conflict emerges. Although familiarity and safety can keep us out of harms way, it can also prevent us from participating in all the positive experiences that life has to offer. The comfort of safety is good for a season, until it no longer helps us move forward with our lives. Then we have a choice to make. Do we stay in a place of comfort, or do we move into the unknown of experience? Psychological growth entails mustering the courage to eventually move out of the comfort zone.

Safety is a basic human need. Safety makes us feel secure, oriented and soothed. Without meeting the psychological need for safety, we would feel unprotected, vulnerable, and out of control. Fear is a warning signal that something is wrong, and we need to protect ourselves from harms way. This is all good and necessary. But many of us use this basic need as a way of protecting ourselves from conflict, trauma, difficult problems, and rocky relationships. This is what I call, "staying in the bubble." We are protective or guarded because it anesthetizes us from the pain of reality. At times, it's necessary to protect ourselves until we can face life head on. For example, if a loved one dies in your family, internally you may immunize yourself from the psychic pain until you are ready to deal with it. In this case, protection is legitimate and it is helpful until you are able to face the reality of what has occurred.

Delayed Reactions to Psychic Pain

I remember making numerous trips to Florida during the time that my father was dying. I recall going back to Florida, where my parents lived, and coping with his terminal illness. After his memorial service, I headed back to Illinois and returned to work. Everyone was so kind and supportive, and they wondered how I was doing with my father's loss. I couldn't figure out why I was doing as well as I was with his death. I was functioning effectively at work and in social situations. Then the Holiday season arrived. Without much warning, I began experiencing depression. I sought medical help because I was having a variety of emotional symptoms that were affecting my ability to cope.

I finally called a therapist friend to find out why I emotionally crashed. After all, I thought I was coping with my father's death effectively. I remember my friend saying to me, "Jim, it's the finality of it all. He's not coming back. There are no more chances to get it right with him." In that moment, the full impact of his death enveloped me. I was grieving for "what could have been." All of the missed opportunities, all the broken promises created by my father came flooding into consciousness. The feelings of sadness and depression were very painful. I kept thinking, how could I flush out the emotions that were now immobilizing me? I began to realize that I was experiencing the pain that I had deflected until I was ready to cope with it.

During the initial stages of grief, we usually run on adrenaline until we start to crumble emotionally. Because I was depressed due to my father's death, I decided to attend a weekend men's retreat as a way of gathering support and working on personal growth issues. One of the activities of the retreat involved flushing out my feelings by writing a letter to my father telling him about the emotional pain that I experienced as his child. Writing that letter was such a difficult project that it took me three sessions to complete it. However, both the group support and the experience of writing the letter helped me bring closure to a difficult chapter in my life. Counselors are not immune from the liabilities of living.

I have counseled many practitioners who have worked in correctional facilities, institutional treatment facilities, and difficult school environments. Many experience the same delayed reaction to psychic pain that I have encountered. Sometimes they wonder why they eventually experience major anxiety attacks, disorientation, and nightmares. Since our mind and body have a way of immunizing us against the psychic pain of trauma, we are safe for a time. But staying on "automatic pilot" is brief, until the full emotional impact of dealing with those who are troubled emerges. We try to stay strong as long as we can. Unfortunately, burn out is on the other side of stress and fatigue from events that may be job related – or they may be the result of years of functioning on automatic pilot in other areas of our lives.

The Magical Beliefs of Childhood

As children we think we have the magical powers to change all that is wrong with the world. We need to believe that we can control problems in order to survive psychologically. For example, sometimes we have parents who are not emotionally healthy. They may lack the capacity to be nurturing, supportive and affirming. In such cases, we perform to please, trying every means to get our parents to act like functional adults. When our efforts fail in getting what we need from our parents, we turn our feelings inward and believe that somehow we are the ones who are defective, not our parents. That way we minimize the pain that results from dealing with them. Many people turn to self-blame as a way of coping and hold the image that our parents will someday change and become the loving people that we always wanted. As we transition to adulthood, many of us maintain this psychic image, believing that people ought to behave the way we want them to respond. Many of us keep striving, pursuing, performing, and fixing in order to fulfill the fantasy of what we want from others. By taking responsibility for our parent's failures, we let them off the hook and minimize the pain regarding how they treated us.

As young children we need the comfort of feeling safe. We tend to gravitate toward that which is familiar and comfortable even when it is dysfunctional. We maintain behavior patterns established by our parents. The safety of our support system makes us feel secure in the midst of an insecure world. Those who experience appropriate parental support and comfort feel grounded. However, as we transition to adulthood, we continue to look for external validation to make us feel secure, while we live in the midst of insecurity. Eventually, the notion of trying to stay secure breaks down as we are faced with ambiguous and challenging problems. Alan Watts, author and philosopher, alludes to this paradox. The more we try to grab onto security, the more we actually feel out of control. "Grabbing for security is like trying to hold water in our hands." Paradoxically, it is only when we accept and embrace insecurity, that we actually become more grounded.

The Courage of Coming Out

Inevitably, if we are to grow and change as adults, the "toothpaste must come out of the tube." We must move gradually out of the bubble. We must confront the challenges, paradoxes, problems, and painful reality of an insecure world. The more we actually accept the call to reality, the easier it becomes to manage the insecurity that goes with it. This is what Watts calls the "wisdom of insecurity." This unfamiliar territory involves experiencing risk and uncomfortable feelings. There is little familiarity in the "wilderness." It can be quite frightening. This is the place where we are struggling to learn and apply new skills for living. It is the uncharted territory in our journey to feel complete.

M. Scott Peck, in his widely acclaimed book, *The Road Less Traveled,* distinguishes between neurotic and legitimate suffering. For me, it represents the difference between being encapsulated in the bubble and stepping out. Staying in the bubble gives us the feeling of security, but prevents us from making our behavioral experience conscious. Our range of emotional response is constricted. We may feel numb, rather than experience the expansiveness of a wide range of emotion. We may feel thwarted, blocked or trapped. Self-destructive behavior can occur when people feel trapped in the bubble. Being encapsulated leaves us vulnerable to that which remains unconscious. As a result of hiding, "psychological leakage" may occur. Unresolved issues of rage and anger, the use of sarcasm, and passive-aggressive behavior are examples of psychological leakage. Unknowingly, things that people say or do while they are in the bubble may wreak havoc on the lives of others.

No one likes to feel the pain that accompanies change and growth, but the option is to remain stagnant, avoiding, procrastinating, deflecting, and blocking everything that opens us to consciousness. M. Scott Peck claims that people avoid problem-solving and learning new skills because they are either too afraid or too lazy, the twin killers of psychological growth. In order to experience growth, one must move forward in challenging ways in spite of utter terror. Many people think that courageous individuals have a special gift, a unique talent for tackling problems. I remind them that no one is immune from the humanity of fear and inertia. If they only knew what Sheldon B. Kopp has said, "No one is any stronger or weaker than anyone else. If you have a hero, look again; you have diminished yourself in some way."

Storing Energy in the Bubble

The bubble is the inner place where we can store the psychic energy of pain. Fred Hanna refers to this place within as the POD, or "phenomenological objective dictate." He uses a therapeutic strategy called the "POD technique" to assist individuals in recognizing and dispelling stored negative energy. This means that we may store within our bodies a constellation of feelings, thoughts, and images that we would prefer to disown. This energy needs to be recognized and objectified in order to minimize its impact. The bubble represents all that is not being made conscious. Hanna has his patients create an image of the constellation of thoughts and feelings being moved outside their body and recognized as a glowing ball. His technique then consists of having the individual get in touch with the complex of feelings which emerge and then having the individual practice letting go of the thoughts and feelings by imagining them as a "white glowing fire" that is disintegrating as they observe the process.

We use various mechanisms to keep our psychic energy in storage. Invariably, people will give off signals that they are in hiding, by employing tactics to minimize the significance of events. I hear comments such as, "My father used a leather strap on me as a kid, but that's over with," or "Yes, my husband beats me, but I still love him so much," and "I've thought about going back to school, but I'm so confused." Excuse making, or deflecting is a convenient way of anesthetizing one against the ravages of pain. For partners who have been abused emotionally or physically, self-doubt is a powerful mechanism for avoiding reality. It keeps anger at bay, and serves the purpose of letting one's abusive partner off the hook. Patients who tell me their painful stories intrigue me. Many people will tell their horrible story with little or no emotion, while I am cringing inside for them. They have protected their emotional state in order to keep their psychic energy intact. Those who blunt their painful emotions are also numb to all the powerful feelings of joy, wonder, and creativity.

For example, I once counseled an adult who displayed little emotion. He complained of being depressed, anxious and unfulfilled. During our sessions his affect was blunted. He exhibited no energy, no passion, with little inflection in his voice. His mannerisms were sluggish and nonchalant. When we communicated he had a blank stare on his face. I wondered if anything I was saying was penetrating his armor.

During our sessions, he would drone on about a litany of complaints. He was very methodical and rigid in the manner in which he communicated. We were not engaged in a dialogue; rather he was talking *at* me. He would bring notes to our sessions and talk from them in a very sterile fashion. He acted as if he was indifferent to the goals we were trying to accomplish in counseling. He complained about the antidepressant medication he was taking, and he obsessed about his health.

His wife had complained about his lack of emotional expressiveness, and therefore I brought the issue up in one of our sessions. Recently his wife's grandmother had died, so I asked him if he had any sorrow about the loss. He indicated that it was his wife's loss, not his, and he had no feelings about her grandmother's death. Pressing him, I asked him if he ever got "caught up" in the emotions of a movie, and he replied that he remained detached from the contents of movies. I asked him if it ever bothered him that he was unable to experience an "emotional life" and he said that he wished that he could share his feelings.

I asked this gentleman if he could remember any childhood recollections of painful memories or disappointments that would account for his shutting down to his feelings. The next thing he did was look at his watch. I asked him, "Are you in a hurry to leave, I noticed you checking your watch." His reply was, "No, I was just checking to see how much time we had left because I could go on endlessly about troublesome events from my past." In deference to time, I asked him to provide me with a few emotionally charged events that affected him from his past. As if he was reading a grocery list, he started conveying to me some of his recollections. First, he cited that his teenaged babysitter molested him when he was five-years old. He never told anyone what had happened. Second, throughout childhood, my client was physically abused by another family member and was afraid to tell his parents due to possible retaliation when attention was drawn to the abuse. Third, when he was in high school he was terrified of public speaking. His lips would shake and he would tremble. His father told him he was being stupid for being so nervous, which just accentuated the problem.

My client shared these personal events in a straightforward, non-emotional manner. When he finished sharing, he responded by saying, "I'm sure you've heard a lot of things worse than this. That's why I hesitated in bringing them to your attention." I thanked him for sharing his memories, and told him it was courageous to do so. I indicated that I now knew him better, because we know one another more effectively through the sharing of our feelings. "Is it any wonder why you have chosen to shut down emotionally and go into hiding?" I replied. The level of emotional wreckage that occurred as a result these events was now out in the open. With recognition, comes the hope of healing. Bringing these traumatic events to the light provides an opening to begin dealing with the hurt, rejection, shame, and disappointment that has kept my client trapped in the pain of the bubble.

Now that my client has recognized and shared his story from the past, we can collaborate on setting goals that will affect his current thoughts, feelings and behavior. Through the sharing of deep feelings, my client will learn that it is acceptable to express his feelings. We will address his father's underlying assumption that it is foolish to be anxious or afraid. Many times people have trouble with permission to express feelings when a parent has criticized them for their emotional responses. I will assist this gentleman in making a connection between maladaptive family-of-origin beliefs and his current condition of withholding feelings, experiencing anxiety, depression and obsessive-compulsive features.

Skillful Work with Trauma

People don't see the reality of things until they are ready to see it. As a therapist I must move slowly as I attempt to poke a hole in the bubble. This means that I search for a "hot button" or underlying belief that has interfered with my client's ability to function adaptively. I help the person recognize the trigger and its impact on current behavior. However, these bubbles of self-protection don't break easily so I must take my time. Sometimes counseling is like peeling an onion - you gently remove one layer at a time. Moving too aggressively will set the patient back and scare them away from change. I must be compassionate and careful, like a skilled surgeon, as I proceed. Taking the props out too quickly will make the person feel too vulnerable and cause him to retreat into his haven of safety. Many people have retreated from therapy because a counselor has moved too quickly when trying to assist the client in uncovering painful truths.

If a therapist is going to assist a client in opening up his painful recollections, the counselor had better be ready to offer emotional support and affirmation. The therapist must also be prepared to offer the individual a meaningful roadmap to healing. A roadmap consists of collaborative goals and plans for implementing change. I deal with a client's maladaptive spontaneous thoughts, cognitive distortions and underlying beliefs. This information is used as the basis for exploration in order to teach the person new ways to respond more adaptively. A comprehensive treatment plan is developed with the client and is signed by both the therapist and counselee. This way there is no misunderstanding about the direction we are heading in our therapeutic venture. It is important to note that taking the "props out" is only the first step toward helping a client find new ways of filling the voids that are left by old ways of thinking and behaving. The vacuum left by a patient's issues must be filled with new and fulfilling ways of relating to the world.

II. REFLECTIONS ON COURAGE

Courage may be defined by those who live outside the bubble as opposed to those who live in it. I like to compare stepping out of the bubble to "wading out into the water." When one wades, they don't thrust themselves in, but slowly move deeper into the flow of things. They wait until they feel safe, defining a path and moving forward. Indeed, people need to be aware of their surroundings as they move forward, picking up cues from the environment. Stepping out of the bubble is not an impulsive act. It is a slow, conscious decision. The good news is that stepping out eventually leads to a new confidence in utilizing skills. Stepping out of the bubble leads to an integration of new abilities into one's lifestyle. The courage to move away from the confinement of the psychological bubble opens a person to endless possibilities for growth.

Using Our Mind and Our Heart

Regardless of conflicting voices, differing rules, and ambiguous perspectives, acting courageously is pretty simple if we dare to trust our heart and mind. M. Scott Peck, renowned psychiatrist and author, jokingly says, "When you make a decision, make it when you're sober and make it again when you're drunk." What I believe he means is that making choices involves both our emotional instincts and our rational mind. If we use both styles of relating, and the answer is consistent, we are probably doing the right thing for us. This process takes courage, because we have no set agenda to guide us. We can't rely exclusively on our church, someone's rules and regulations, or our family and friends to assist us. No external opinions replace the need to figure out what it means to do the appropriate thing for us. The choices are endless and ours to make.

Sometimes we pay a price for doing the courageous thing. There are those who will assail us for making courageous choices. For some, jobs are lost, partners withdraw, and friends disappear. Some people won't like the choices we make. When the boy in the plastic bubble stepped out of that bubble against the tide of his family and doctor, his courage to live cost him his life. Most decisions that we make certainly are not so risky that they put our life in jeopardy. But decisions we make can certainly create consequences. The byproduct of the decisions we make can affect others in positive or negative ways. We must learn to choose. There is no life, no love, without risk. It's the fear of living, of loving, that binds us.

The Courage to Change

Acting to change our behavior is a courageous choice. After significant reflection and possible heartache, we must choose. If we choose not to make a choice, we suffer the consequences. We stay enveloped in the bubble, not conscious of a plan or path to release ourselves from the tyranny of the past. The past is not always *in the past.* The past may be carried with us in the here-and-now. If there are dusty corners in our emotional closet, they need to be swept out. Sweeping out remnants of difficult past experiences makes room for new and more meaningful experiences. All of us claim we want this, but only some choose to do what's necessary to change the way we deal with our psychological history.

As the old saying goes, "history tends to repeat itself." Some of us can see that pattern with problems that tend to be intergenerational. We look in the mirror and we see traces of our parents' or grandparent's behavior, and we are not always happy with what that means. But individually, we must make a personal promise to courageously modify patterns of behavior that continue to be self-defeating. Our history of self-sabotaging behavior can be altered. It merely takes the commitment to do it. There are many supportive people willing to help any of us. We need to mobilize the courage to reach out. Behaving in the same ways that don't work is folly; and yet there are many who repeat the same patterns over and over again.

Maintaining Maladaptive Patterns

An example is a woman client of mine who is in highly dysfunctional relationship with her partner. Her partner, by her admission, is highly abusive. He is intimidating, raging and controlling. She fears his wrath and yet she stays in the relationship. She claims that when his mood is elevated, he is extremely romantic.

She derives pleasure in feeding off the manic behavior that he displays. She loves the manic, expansive side of his personality and refuses to give him up. Although she continues to get hurt and is disappointed by her partner, she maintains the relationship anyway. They have had a pattern of breaking off the relationship and reconciling. The drama of upheaval continues as she maintains her relationship addiction, hanging on to the comfort of discomfort.

William Glasser, noted psychiatrist and school consultant, discusses with teachers the pattern of maintaining dysfunctional relationships with students. In his presentations he will ask teachers, "How many of you feel like you are spinning your wheels in the classroom?" He admonishes teachers to quit doing the same old things that don't work. Issues such as classroom management, discipline, style of communicating, and student evaluation procedures may need reassessment. At a presentation for teachers, I remember Glasser remarking, "Instead of irritating the hell out of kids for eight hours a day, try something new." He further explains that if what you are doing is not working, move in a different direction. Teaching is an art, so become pragmatic.

The Courage to be Decisive

People who live in the bubble are indecisive. One of the hallmarks of non-risk- takers is their inability to choose. It doesn't matter whether it is a big decision or minor one, such people lack the courage to make a choice. Have you ever been with someone while dining out who takes an inordinate amount of time choosing from the menu? They agonize as they contemplate the significance of what to eat. Making a wrong choice for the anxiety driven decision-maker appears catastrophic. The primary fear appears to be the misfortune of making a mistake. According to those who are decision-phobic, mistakes must be avoided at all costs. Making a mistake is considered a personal failure and it can't be tolerated. It takes courage to feel comfortable about making a decision that may involve the potential for risk and mistakes.

Many people are terrified of making mistakes. The origins of this fear may stem from parenting issues during childhood. One's parents may have been either overfunctioning adults, not allowing their children to make their own decisions; or the parents may have been highly controlling, critical, and intimidating; or they may have been "absent parents". In any case, the underlying message was, "Others can do for you much better than you can do for yourself." Powerful words originating out of childhood can be tools that affect people's opinions, choices, and behavior. They can rob a child of courage to function independently.

We make decisions based upon the best information available at the time the choice is made. One can always second-guess a decision, but I tell my patients that there are to be no regrets. There is no such thing as a calculated risk. All risks ultimately involve jumping off the deep end and hoping for the best. There are no guarantees, no assurances in this business of stepping out of the bubble. One must forgive oneself for being less than perfect and learn to live with the consequences of one's actions. Taking personal responsibility for change is essential and it is courageous.

In order to assist indecisive people, I ask them, "What is the worst thing that can happen if you make a mistake?" Having clients realistically evaluate potential outcomes of their behavior helps people get things in perspective. The concept of *making* a decision needs to be viewed apart from the decision to be made. I tell patients that if they *choose,* they are courageous win or lose. Making decisions empower us and give us the courage to make future choices. Once a decision is made, mistakes don't seem so debilitating. A choice that doesn't go according to plans can be changed. Once we have internalized the power of decision-making, we can always make new choices. No one decision seems so dramatic. It's through changing behaviors such as decision-making that we grow and develop.

The Courage to Heal or Let Go of Relationships

I believe all of us need to become comfortable with our personal story, as aspects of it may constitute our legacy. The qualities we possess, the nature of our relationships, and the way we behave toward others leaves an imprint. Hopefully, part of our story involves demonstrating courage in the face of adversity. Hopefully it involves establishing more meaningful relationships as we grow older. Hopefully we have repaired relationships in our family to the degree that we can, and have employed forgiveness as a guide to healing. By forgiveness, I do not mean the "cheap grace" that many embrace. I mean coming to terms with the difficulties that arise out of human connections and learning to let go and forgive our strained relationships and the ways others have hurt and disappointed us.

Many times I explore with people the issues involved in making major relationship decisions. A patient may be ready to explore giving up the illusion of "what could have been within his marriage." Giving up a fantasy is difficult. Most of us hold onto an image until it becomes too unbearable. Then we begin the grieving process. A partner's inner voice may be saying things like, "This is not fair; what did I do to deserve this; I feel like a failure; it's all my fault; why can't she be the way I want her to be." Once the unrealistic image is addressed, the partner is ready to step outside the bubble. This is a painful process, but there is usually a sense of peace, a matter of "knowing" that goes with it.

With big decisions, such as dissolving a marriage, choosing is very difficult. Sometimes, no matter how bad the marriage, it may take years for a partner to trust his instincts. Our instincts always tell us to move forward, whatever that may mean for us. We are challenged to chart an unfamiliar course. Such decisions, as ending a marriage, involve taking responsibility, admitting failures and moving on.

Moving on may involve hurting our partner, not intentionally, but because the loving thing is to admit that reconciliation is no longer an option. It is a step towards personal integrity. Having tried all remedies, including spiritual and psychological support, there may be no recourse. Nobody can illuminate what is no longer there. But with finality, comes courage, grieving and ultimately relief. Who can fault you for doing what your inner voice tells you is necessary? As painful as the process becomes, you have stepped outside of the bubble.

Seeing Things with Perfect Clarity

Staying outside of the bubble and experiencing life the way it really is takes supreme courage. One of the goals in the pilgrimage of psychotherapy is to see things clearly. We all have mechanisms for distorting the truth. Psychotherapy, if it is effective aims at illuminating for the client that which is true. We must seek the truth, no matter where it takes us. As I mentioned previously, people use all kinds of defense mechanisms to avoid facing the pain of reality. Minimization, catastrophizing, manipulation, deflection, victimization, and "numbing out" are examples. These resistant mechanisms are designed to keep individuals in the comfort zone, rather than stepping out. It is the job of the therapist to appropriately "frustrate" the client into giving up the impasse. Fritz Perls, Gestalt therapist, used the term "frustrating the client" to mean making the client take responsibility for thoughts and feelings without making excuses. The job is easier if the therapist is soothing, comforting, and affirming with his patients. But resistance must be met without allowing the client to foster a pattern of dependence with the therapist. A client may feign weakness and confusion in order to avoid deep feelings and such manipulation must be directly challenged.

Most of my patients come to see me because they don't want to maintain their negative thoughts and feelings. They want to come out of hiding. It takes a great deal of courage to engage in therapy because there are no guarantees. How do we know we'll end up liking what we see as we expose ourselves to awareness? "Maybe I won't like what I see or other's won't like what they see; maybe the psychic pain will be more than I can tolerate and I'll disappear; what if I don't have what it takes." One must leave the bubble to find out. There is no other way. It's what stays hidden, unconscious that leads to destructive thinking and maladaptive behavior.

Courage Has Its Price

Going through the wilderness is not easy. It requires a commitment to psychological healing and growth. Those who choose to hide, live in the void of emotional constrictedness. Living in a vacuum emotionally means that the individual lives with a narrow range of feelings. The emotionally expressive person has a wider repertoire of feelings, being able to experience deep sadness, as well as a heightened sense of joy and wonder. Emotional expressiveness comes as a result of moving *through* one's feelings no matter how troublesome. The paradox is that the more we flush out the dark side of the psyche, the more we are able to appreciate and experience the wondrous side of our emotions.

Going through the wilderness means reexperiencing and reinterpreting reality and finding new hope. It means feeling the full impact of any experience either past or present that has affected us in an unhealthy manner. Because we may have filtered our pain over traumatic events, perceiving those events in an accurate fashion may be highly difficult, but necessary. Our pain must be experienced the way it really is. Having someone to support you through this process is essential. As we let down our guard, we need those who can affirm, nurture and soothe us as we move along the rocky road toward healthy functioning.

In order to experience psychological healing, one must occasionally go through the "dark night of the soul." This means that the patient must gather the strength and courage to experience the full emotional impact of reality. Most of us have a way of filtering out bits and pieces of psychic pain. If we have been involved with traumatic events as a child, we find ways to distort reality to keep us safe. We may take the blame, we may try to fix people or events, act in pleasing ways, self-medicate, or we may become oppositional.

These strategies may have worked to help us survive as a child, but we pay a price for our silence. As an adult, if we are courageous, we begin the process of re-experiencing these fragments of childhood pain that bound us in the bubble. In adulthood, there is no longer shelter from our past. Our past will follow us around in a destructive way if we don't deal with it. We may project our past in a way that begins to take its toll on our family members. Anxiety, panic, blame, and anger may be manifested in a way that does harm to our most intimate family members. We may have personally numbed out to our past and then spewed its contents on those we love the most. Most of us come to a point where we ponder, "Do I stay in hiding, or do I come out and face the emotional ramifications of my issues?"

In some ways, stepping out of the bubble makes life more complex. Once we have left the safety net, problems must be confronted. There are no longer simple solutions to problems. There is no normative way of viewing the world. We look at life out of a different set of lenses. There are polarities, tensions, ambiguities, paradoxes, and multiple ways of viewing problems. At first, this change in direction may make us feel disoriented and insecure. Some years ago, I was the patient in my own personal counseling. One particular session I had with my counselor was very intense. The session was highly emotionally charged and I left the office feeling quite fatigued and disoriented. On my way home I lost a sense of where I was going directionally. I panicked. I could not pick up spatial cues that would help me figure out where I was located. I was lost, somewhere. Finally, the episode passed and I recovered a sense of spatial relationship. This experience is not unusual at the onset of deep, significant emotional upheaval.

The Courage to Confront

Those who step out of the bubble open up to developing assertive patterns of communicating. I define assertiveness as expressing one's needs and wants in a way that does not intentionally hurt others. A counselor friend of mine once told me that there is nothing admirable about avoiding hurt. Hurt is an inevitable byproduct of making difficult decisions. I'm always amazed at couples that come to see me for marriage counseling. I often hear at the onset of counseling, "I'm not sure what's wrong with our relationship because my wife and I never argue or fight." I call this the Couple Bubble! As long as they insulate themselves, they don't have to deal with conflict. Staying in the bubble keeps them from experiencing the struggle for intimacy.

Handling conflict is a process that is foreign to many of us. We lack the experience of promoting understanding through telling our partners what is bothering us. Rather, we passively stockpile our feelings and let them leak out in ways that are destructive to our relationships. The use of sarcasm is a perfect example. Couples use sarcasm as a way of dancing around significant issues. This process helps minimize the significance of conflict. It's like two stallions circling around each other in the corral. But what role-modeling did most of us have for constructively sharing our true feelings with our friends and partners? As individuals we often can assert ourselves with our business partners, but feel lost in communicating honestly and openly with those closest to us. This pattern exists because it is more frightening to be vulnerable with the people with whom we are most intimate.

In order to be assertive, one must let go of the power of other's approval and disapproval. At times, all of us are afraid to share our deepest feelings because of the negative reaction we might get from others. We assume or anticipate that our friends will judge us for being true to who we are. In the 1970's, Father John Powell of Loyola University of Chicago reflected on this dilemma in a book, *Why am I Afraid to Tell You Who I Am?* None of us like the feeling of being vulnerable, although it appears that the most empowered people are those who can choose to be vulnerable when necessary. I believe that vulnerability in concert with empowerment leads to psychological wholeness. Sometimes I tell people to think of assertiveness the way television detective Columbo responds during his investigations. Columbo responds by saying, "Help me understand something, sir? And, by the way, can you explain that to me again? Just one more question," he responds. Assertiveness involves respecting and valuing the promotion of understanding. It is a dialogue, with true appreciation for differences in opinion. It also means learning to say no. It means setting boundaries that are acceptable and not being manipulated into changing them. It means the possibility of disappointing others, and learning to live with their disapproval. It means respecting oneself enough to stand firm on what you want and need without getting caught up in the burden of others feelings.

Courage to Trust Our Instincts

Several years ago my wife and I were in New Orleans for a conference. One morning we made a stop at a pharmacy in the city. While we were perusing the store, two young men entered and made their way to separate places in the store. I watched their anxiousness, their hypervigilance, and that was enough for me. I could feel the tension mounting. I didn't know whether they wanted something from my wife and me or from the store clerk. I wasn't about to wait to find out. I clutched my wife's hand and we immediately left the premise. Sometimes there is a "knowing" which comes with experience that tells you that trouble is brewing. Learning to trust your instincts can be helpful in protecting one from harm and establishing appropriate boundaries with others. People in the bubble discount their instincts.

Discounting the obvious conveniently keeps people in a pattern of avoidance. They don't have to stick their neck out or assert themselves in any way. This pattern is convenient, but there is a price to pay. A number of years ago I heard the author M. Scott Peck speak to a group of mental health professionals in Chicago. He talked about having chronic neck pain and how troublesome it was. After many medical tests, and self-refection, he came to the conclusion that his problem was partially due to his inability to "stick his neck out." One of my patients had a similar problem. Whenever he caught himself trying to fix everyone's problems at home, and failed to assert his own needs, his neck stiffened up. He kept getting caught up in the burden of his family's feelings while ignoring his own.

The core issue is one of permission. Discounters are unable to give themselves permission to experience or express their feelings. They may have very clear goals and needs, but will minimize them. The underlying assumption is, "I am not worth it, and therefore I will never succeed in realizing my dreams and aspirations." Many times these clients feel guilty for pursuing goals that their parents never reached. They live with a fear of success as if they don't deserve to achieve what they desire. They typically anticipate failure and set up a self-defeating pattern. If friends or family say things that irritate them, this individual will ignore instincts to respond and succumb to irrational assertions from others. Later, this person will regret not having responded and will feel resentful toward the perpetrator. Teaching people to trust their instincts and to act on them in appropriate ways is always a goal of therapy. Helping them to develop skills in rationally responding to maladaptive thinking is another goal.

III. REFLECTIONS OF AUTHENTICTY

Developing authenticity is an important goal of therapy. It involves role modeling and supporting clients in being true to who they are. It is learning to accept oneself with all the warts. That's what the counseling process is all about. It's allowing people to let their guard down and tell you about their hidden feelings. People have trouble sharing their secret feelings because they are afraid of being that vulnerable. They are afraid they will disappoint others or that they will be discounted. Stepping out of the bubble and learning to be transparent is an important feature of the counseling process. A client may be saying, "I want you to accept the part of me that appears unacceptable, because it's all I have." The healing comes when the person realizes that their less than admirable side can be integrated into the whole. "I am good enough. I can live in my own skin."

Authentic people demonstrate integrity. They are honest with themselves and others and are respected for their values and convictions. They are not afraid to tell you who they are. There is a transparency about the way they communicate. You really know these people. You don't have to *try* to get to know them. They radiate enthusiasm and positive energy. They understand their limitations and utilize their strengths. They are a joy to be around. Authentic people are relaxed because they are not afraid of what others think. They recognize that their inner voice is more convincing and important than all the other voices in their sphere of influence. They are not afraid to make difficult decisions, after recognizing what the consequences might be. They stay out of the bubble because life is more enriching and fulfilling.

Authenticity Involves Integrating

Authentic, grounded people are not swallowed up by any one part of themselves. Although I believe we all have a centered self, I am not sure that I believe that the human psyche is always unified. We have various subpersonalities that clamor for attention. Most theories of personality acknowledge the polarities of the human psyche. For example, Gestalt therapy makes reference to the "top dog/underdog" polarity. Jungian psychology has its archetypes. Freud made reference to the id, ego, and superego. Transactional analysis referred to the adult, parent and child.

Subpersonalities (energy systems) crystallize and emerge early in life as a way of coping with various needs and wants. We all wear different faces, such as the critic, the pusher-driver, the vulnerable child and the creative adult. Occasionally in counseling, I will ask people to give their different faces or energy systems names and they typically have no problem identifying them. C*razy Catherine, Humble Howie, Little Petey,* and *Theresa the Tiger* are examples. These names represent energy that may be expressed depending on certain situations that trigger responses. Problems arise when any one subpersonality takes control and steers the individual. Sometimes we say that these people are "swallowed up" by a subpersonality. When this occurs, the only inner voice that one hears is that which represents the subpersonality. If the critic takes over, it is full of *musts, oughts, shoulds,* or other critical mandates. We actually become the critic, like a parent who has lost his mental compass. However, those who step outside the bubble, and are not overpowered by any one energy system, are like the conductor of an orchestra. They are able to coordinate the strings, the brass, the woodwinds, and percussion. Everything is integrated, coordinated and works in harmony. I like to compare the grounded, authentic and integrated self to the maestro, one who makes beautiful music.

Being authentic means having all of one's energy systems working in harmony. There is a "grounded self" that is able to coordinate and integrate each subpersonality. Sometimes I conduct subpersonality treatment techniques with clients. I work with clients energy systems, based on treatment modalities such as the *Voice Dialogue* method of Hal and Sidra Stone. For example, a client may have a dependent and independent side of their personality that is in conflict. I will move the client to a different place in my office and deal directly with the energy systems creating difficulties. In this case, I will have the client take on the energy of the "dependent child" and speak directly about that part. I will explore questions such as, "Tell me how you function in my client's life? What keeps you from acting in more assertive ways?" Then I will have the client move again and take on the "independent adult" subpersonality. I might ask, "What makes you want to act more independently? What scares you about functioning in a more independent fashion?" When I am finished speaking with each part I will bring the individual back to his original seating position and process the experience out of a place of client awareness. I might ask, "What have you learned about these energy systems? Do you get any idea as to why they are at war with each other? How can we help them cooperate with each other so that you feel integrated? The purpose of energy work is to help the client learn to identify with the conscious contents of each subpersonality and then to detach from its contents. This leads to more authenticity, integration, coordination and synthesis of the personality.

<h2 style="text-align:center">No One is Any Stronger or Weaker than Anyone Else</h2>

Those who are authentic understand their limits. They perform within a set of reasonable boundaries. They are not unrealistic about expectations for themselves and others. They do not get caught up in the burden of other's feelings. They are able to stay appropriately detached. They are neither too weak nor arrogant. They are not overly impressed by their own success and material possessions, and do not compare their worth or financial status with others. They treat people with respect regardless of one's economic status or financial resources.

Is it better to be honest about what you think and feel, or better to experience the illusion of safety? Those who choose to be authentic have no room for the comfort zone. I believe that helping people become authentic is a major goal of therapy. Learning to be authentic means being true to your real self. As I mentioned earlier, Sheldon B. Kopp has said, "No one is any stronger or any weaker than anyone else." The moment we think we are, we have deceived ourselves. Authenticity involves learning to be comfortable in our own skin. Authentic people live rather effortlessly, without striving, anticipating, or comparing themselves to others.

The Courage to Discover Your Identity

One of the most courageous steps an individual can make is revealing troublesome personal issues. Years ago I had a client who admitted that she was struggling with her sexual identity. A close friend of hers referred her to me due to her stress and a lack of confidence. Over time we have been able to minimize her anxiety and help her with assertiveness skills on the job. Social anxiety has still been an overriding concern that has impaired her development in relationships. When I would ask her about developing friendships, particularly male-female ones, she would become subdued. We explored her history of dating and it was insignificant. She was uncomfortable with the males she had dated throughout high school and college. After several sessions, she finally responded with courage and great conflict, "I am not sure I have ever been attracted to men." "Are you more attracted to women?" I asked. "Yes, I guess that's true, but I've never defined myself sexually."

Here was a woman over forty years old grappling with her sexual orientation for the first time. She had never told anybody about this conflict and confusion nor could she imagine disclosing these feelings with others. Her anguish and confusion were complicated by the fact that the church she belonged to was strongly opposed to homosexuality. For the first time she had admitted that she was not comfortable in her own skin. Can you imagine what that must be like? To feel the tug of betrayal of negative religious sanctions? To feel thwarted from experiencing the truth about the nature of one's being? My role had been to guide her toward being authentic, true to her experience. As a therapist, what other option do I have? Do I tell her to deny the reality of her experience? We spent a long time on helping this client to develop a spiritual connection with a church group that honors those who are gay. She remained hesitant to make this contact because it validates what she has been denying most of her life. Any form of disclosure of sexual orientation will be an issue of great sensitivity for this woman.

Promoting Authenticity in Counseling

Being authentic and a person of integrity mean that we are flexible. We step out of the bubble, look at all the options and evidence and proceed to do the right thing. Some psychotherapists believe that the primary goal of therapy is to promote authenticity. Counselors must model authenticity in the therapeutic process. Many times I tell people that in order for me to role model authenticity, I must take my clinical hat off before walking in my office. They understand what I mean. We all play roles in life, but many times our roles can actually distract us from carrying out our mission in a professional manner. I try to think about my perception of a typical therapist; those who are detached, passive and without humor. I try to make sure that I create a perception in therapy that makes my clients feel comfortable with me.

One of my past clients once remarked in the heat of conjoint therapy, "I can't stand mental health workers!" Rather than become defensive, I asked him to explain the nature of his experience with mental health professionals. I began to validate his perspective because he had some excellent points to make. He felt that his kids had gotten bogged down in their experience with a litany of mental health workers because of his wife's concerns for the children. He felt that none of the counselors had honored his viewpoint about the value of counseling. The more I listened and validated him, paradoxically the more he accepted the counseling process. He came to believe that being a counselor was more than displaying a robotic style with predetermined responses to every person and every situation. But how does the therapist facilitate this process of developing authenticity?

There are certain qualities or conditions that the counselor must exude in order for authenticity to blossom. The counselor must role model qualities which Carl Rogers, founder of Client-Centered Therapy, noted such as genuineness, acceptance, promoting a soothing environment, being nurturing, and affirming. These conditions foster the therapeutic climate for change. Without these conditions demonstrated by the counselor, it is difficult to build a therapeutic alliance. Collaboration calls for trust, and these qualities promote the kind of trust necessary to facilitate therapeutic change.

The Small Person Syndrome

Some people lack authenticity and I refer to them as "small people." They are difficult to deal with because they have blocked many issues about competency from consciousness. They overcompensate by trying to act overly important. In the corporate world, these are the leaders who like to micromanage, who use boss management techniques, and believe in a hierarchal system of organization. They can be arrogant, pushy, overcontrolling and detached. They often have their needs met by telling others what to do and how to do it. They don't role model or lead by example. They believe they are well versed on all subjects and want others to follow their lead. They are highly rigid, critical, and use coercive techniques to control employees rather than use affirmation and coaching.

Years ago I worked in a school as Director of Guidance and Counseling. Two administrators who had many years of educational experience hired me. They were aware of my previous work and expertise in the field of school guidance. Their management style was to empower me by giving me the freedom to create a department that would be an asset for the school. At that time, I also worked at a university as an adjunct faculty member teaching counselor education classes. I used our school guidance program as a model for excellence within our class for comparison purposes. After several years, both of my educational administrators decided to retire. Prior to leaving, they commended me for turning around a guidance program that was in disarray.

The school district conducted a "nation-wide search" to replace my superiors. The district finally settled on two in-house individuals who served as deans of students to take the positions. Soon after that, I started work under this new administrative team, getting the scheduling program started. I was called into my new immediate superior's office and she proceeded to inform me of a litany of new policies and procedures that would govern my department and my job. She had created an entirely new format for the counseling department without the courtesy of consulting with me as department chairman. She had a new, comprehensive plan for my department and she was going to execute it.

The word got out about the "master plan" for running the counseling department and my colleagues were furious because none of us had been included in the planning. Morale plummeted and my co-workers began doing only the minimum amount of work required of them. The enthusiasm for our work was no longer present.

One possible explanation for why these kinds of things can happen is that when people try to act 'big', they lack authenticity. When you are new to a position, you have two choices. One is to seek assistance and support in the process of leading others, or to pretend you know it all even though everyone knows you don't. Small people project their insecurities onto others. They try to make others feel small, and in doing so, they attempt to elevate themselves.

Individuals who demonstrate strength and experience can be intimidating to small people. In order to maintain their fragile sense of self, small people try to boost their self-esteem at the expense of others. They may attack and demean those who pose a threat to their self-image. When small people feel threatened there is no stopping them. They will do whatever it takes to attack and demean those that they perceive as threatening. The more resistance they sense, the more they go on the attack. Such people, with their fragile sense of self, thrive on the ability to gain power and control over those who they attempt to manage. My psychiatrist friend calls such managers compulsive bureaucrats. They are focused on the minutiae, and they have no other style of relating. They lack authenticity.

IV. REFLECTIONS ON THEMES OF THERAPY

As a therapist, you never want to deflate the bubble without supporting the client through the painful process of change. Educating people about the counseling process which may involve revealing uncomfortable feelings is helpful. Suggesting ways of refocusing energy through various outlets including exercise, socialization, visual imagery, meditation, and message therapy are beneficial in softening the impact of the emotional release, which occurs as a byproduct of therapy. Reassuring the client that you will support and comfort her through the counseling journey is essential.

The Commitment to Change

At the onset of counseling, I tell patients that making progress involves time and commitment. Until we actually get involved in their issues, little do individuals realize the significance of the need for commitment. I had a male adult who came to me for counseling. He called and said it was an emergency. I worked him in the same day he called. He was quite agitated and anxious when he arrived. He came with his parents even though he was an adult. The client agreed that meeting with his parents would be helpful to therapy. Therefore, I had the client sign a release so that his parents could visit with me first. They were able to give me a significant amount of background information. Then it was time for my client. I educated the client about time involvement and commitment to therapy. During therapy this client revealed how afraid he was because he would cycle into a mood that would make him feel like killing himself or others. He was afraid he would act on his impulses.

Since this client was obviously in danger of hurting himself or others, I had him voluntarily admitted to a mental health facility in order to get him stabilized. As I brought the parents into my office to hear my assessment, I kept thinking about what I had told my patient about commitment and also the courage it took to accept my evaluation of his condition. Both he and his parents complied and I commended them for taking a step outside the bubble. Now we could proceed with on-going therapy once he was discharged from the hospital.

People will say they want to change, but sometimes do not recognize the impact of such a decision. Those who move forward and make progress are those who stop whining and start working. Self-exploration is hard work and takes a high degree of commitment and courage. Many people are not willing to make the sacrifices necessary to implement change. They don't want to give up their addictions, their self-defeating behavior, their messy relationships, and the illusions of youth. If you try to touch any of these areas many people will balk. They are saying without words, "Don't go there with me, it's my security blanket."

This does not occur without a great deal of resistance. But if you keep pulling on the blanket long enough, many patients will let it go and grieve all that it stands for. It stands for the illusion of youth, all of our old habits, worn out relationships, and fear of growing old and facing the reality of mortality. Ironically, it stands for all the familiar security found in dysfunctional beliefs and behaviors.

Recognition, the Beginning of Change

When people act out negative behaviors due to a lack of awareness, I call it "leakage." People use subtle forms of behavior to hurt their significant others and then are puzzled by the reactions. Some time ago a gentleman came to see me because his wife told him that he used sarcasm as a way of displaying anger toward her. He appeared clueless about the manner in which his behavior was affecting his wife. "I just don't agree with her about my anger issues," he replied. I asked him to describe to me the nature of the relationship that he had with his father during childhood. His father was born in Germany and came to the United States as a boy. His father maintained the old world mentality that "children were to be seen, not heard." The other assumption this client held was that "big boys don't cry." His father was an intimidating, dominating figure when he was at home. "Did you feel thwarted with respect to sharing your feelings at home?" "You bet," he responded. "Do you see any connection between the way you related with your father and how you communicate with your wife?" "I'm very passive, but I believe I stuff my feelings." "Yes you do, and the way you express your resentment is in the form of sarcasm. You learned your lessons well from childhood." My client was now able to make that which was hidden open to awareness. Recognition or awareness is the first step in moving toward behavioral change.

As M. Scott Peck states, every client comes to therapy with a psychic map. This map is the client's psychological story that he brings to counseling. It is based on a constellation of thoughts and feelings that form a pattern of behavior. The map may be outdated or distorted. It may need revision. It is the goal of the therapist to enlarge one's map to take into consideration new ideas and behaviors. Resistance often comes at the thought of change. It is the therapist's objective to gently poke a hole in the psychological bubble so that the client can see a glimmer of daylight. It is bringing issues to the light that affects change. The challenge is getting people to want to develop awareness. The problem with the light is that it is not selective. It shines on both our good qualities and the dusty corners of our personality. It is the "shadow self" as the Jungian psychologist's proclaim, which needs the light.

We are afraid to expose the darkness to the light because it makes us feel vulnerable. We are uncomfortable with our own vulnerability because we are afraid that we, or others may not like who we are. I had a client who had divorced an abusive husband and was now in a relationship with a very affirming, nurturing gentleman. The intimacy in the new relationship opened her up to the sunshine, but it also illuminated issues that needed healing. The contrast between the openness of the new relationship, and the guardedness of her prior relationship seemed confusing. The new relationship served as a catalyst in bringing the shadows of her life to the forefront. Now she had to deal with issues of abandonment, hurt and disappointment. She needed to learn that she deserved to be loved, that it was permissible to share loving feelings and to learn to view vulnerability as a friend, not an enemy. She was frightened by the risk of loving. She had never experienced much intimacy in her marriage relationship, so this new experience felt foreign. It was time to explore and disconnect from the feelings of the past. Such change takes time and patience.

It is the work of the therapist to help the others make a connection between troublesome "hot buttons" and the nature of one's current behavior. It is the therapist's responsibility to assist the client in making troublesome issues more conscious. The counselor may meet some resistance in moving others in the direction of change. Helping the client to step out of the bubble is difficult work and calls for skillful attention to the body language and emotional reactions of the client. It is a sensitive process to move the people out of shelter and into awareness. When clients minimize what appears to be sensitive information, the therapist must consider ways of getting at the emotional content of the story. Like delicate surgery, the therapist attempts to refocus the client's attention on issues of intensity. Helping others to become aware of the fact that they have minimized significant emotional content is imperative. Many clients will tell the therapist that their baggage is "history" and does not need further exploration. It is my responsibility to make sure that clients have established emotional closure on family-of-origin issues so that emotional history does not affect their everyday functioning.

Patients who resist the process of exploring issues involving deep feelings tend to stay constricted emotionally. By that I mean that they tend to be rather stoic, hostile, and distant. It's not uncommon for one partner to remark to me, "I don't know this person anymore." Deflecting problems tends to create maladaptive behavior. Deflectors tend to be rigid, unreasonably logical, argumentative, defensive, insensitive, and repeaters of dysfunctional patterns of behavior. For example, it is not uncommon for patients who experienced verbal or physical abuse as children to gravitate toward careers where they provide caretaking for others. Teachers, mental health professionals, and those in the field of corrections are many times playing out their own history of abuse in an environment that may illuminate abusiveness.

Several years ago I had a mental health provider who came to see me because he was stressed out due to working in an adolescent inpatient treatment program. He was the "go-to-guy" in his sphere of influence. All his colleagues looked up to him for his skills in "restraining" and doing "take downs" on unruly kids. He had lived through similar trauma in his own childhood. Now he was reliving it in the context of his job. His co-workers were exploiting him because he was a master at coping with trauma. They looked to him to bridle the defiant teens under their care. It finally became too much for him and he began to break down emotionally. When he first came to see me he was distraught, fatigued, depressed, and highly anxious. It was time to break the cycle; to give up the need to be a self-sacrificing hero. He was losing himself in the process of expending so much energy and time assisting troubled kids. He finally learned to set boundaries for himself and let others do what they needed to do to help out. He finally learned that he could delegate responsibility and that he was dispensable. It was quite a relief for him to learn that others would be there to support him.

The Fear of Connecting

Many of my patients suffer from social anxiety or social phobia as it is now called. These clients are terrified of making emotional and social contact with others. They maintain excuses for avoiding a connection with others, fearing the notion of reaching out to others. I sometimes hear, "I've been rejected too much; they're not my kind; those kids think they are too cool", and so on. Excuse making creates an artificial barrier that keeps the avoider on the perimeter of life experience. Because of their maladaptive perceptions, socially anxious people give off negative energy and accomplish their goal of hiding from others. They might ask me, "What would I say to others?" which is a signal of the level of their anxiety and can give me an indication of the level of aloneness they feel about the prospects of connecting with others. Most have never had a role model for what psychotherapist Fritz Perls called "contactfulness."

Those who are socially anxious are experts at self-monitoring. They tend to be overly sensitive to their perception of what others think about them. Their underlying assumption about life is, "I don't deserve to be loved, because I am not good enough for you." Once these people can develop the courage to step out of the self-monitoring (self-centeredness) and explore the external world, then the excitement begins. Slowly, one may wade into the water, checking for sharks and other dangerous critters, and begin asking simple questions that will help her relate to others better. At first it feels awkward as a client grapples with what to say. I always tell anxious clients that people love it when you act interested in their life experiences. How many times have people really shown an interest in whom you are or what you like to do?

When I was about to meet my father-in-law, my wife reminded me that he should have been a "professional interrogator." "I warn you, he will ask you every question imaginable." What she failed to realize is that I welcomed his involvement in my life because I was not used to anyone caring that much. How wonderful it is to be able to talk about yourself! I found a friend. If a social phobic follows the advice of Gestalt psychotherapist Fritz Perls and "gets out of his head and into his senses," things will begin to change. Confidence builds, personal energy becomes more positive, and a pattern of acceptance and willingness to make contact with others will emerge.

People who lack social confidence have a difficult time trusting their instincts. If they feel something, or think something, they immediately discard it as not credible. All of us have a tendency to refuse to act on feelings, thoughts or sensations because we don't trust ourselves. Those with social anxiety have a habit of not trusting their experience. They have learned that what's inside is not acceptable, or trustworthy. Sometimes family history has created a pattern, by teaching anxious people to thwart their feelings. Many parents have been masters at teaching their youngsters the technique of discounting their emotional experience. Many socially anxious clients have felt intimidated and controlled by overbearing parents. They developed a hypersensitivity to sharing their thoughts and feelings because they were not given an opportunity to promote understanding through sharing. These families operate in a frozen vacuum when it comes to expressing feelings. There is an underlying assumption that the expression of deep feeling is to be avoided at all costs. Therefore, children develop a pattern of internalizing feelings rather than expressing them appropriately.

Counseling with socially phobic people involves teaching them assertiveness skills, building confidence, helping clients set appropriate limits, and coaching them in successful ways of communicating with others. It also involves helping people learn to risk making emotional contact with others rather than "measuring" their words. In order to be an effective communicator, one must learn to be appropriately vulnerable by taking the risk to be emotionally expressive without worrying about the approval or disapproval of others.

The Permission to Feel

I had a gentleman come to see me who was suffering with a massive amount of anxiety. He was bogged down with guilt and self-blame because he was attracted to a young lady at work, although he was married. Occasionally he had flirted with this woman, but that was the extent of any romantic feelings or behavior. "Have you acted on your feelings in any way that would make your wife uncomfortable?" As he said this was not the case, I explained that many times feelings come unbidden. I admonished him to allow for inner-permission to experience his flirtatious feelings, as he had been browbeating himself for doing it. "If you feel your feelings they will have less power over you," I replied. He was confused by my suggestion because he was used to thinking that experiencing feelings could cause one to lose control. He was afraid that experiencing his feelings would lead to inappropriate behavior. Many times, just the opposite is true. It is when we thwart our feelings that we tend to lose control. Holding onto our feelings too tightly can set us up for emotional and behavioral problems.

His guilt feelings were another issue to be addressed. Most people don't struggle with true guilt. I define true guilt as going against one's convictions, betraying one's inner self. It is the process of missing the mark, and usually calls for amends to be made to those we have harmed. The majority of guilt is what psychotherapist Fritz Perls called "disguised resentment." This is false guilt. We substitute one feeling for another. It is easier to feel guilty than to come to terms with our anger and resentment. False guilt is when you let people have power over you and you resent them for having that control. My client was resentful of his wife who he felt had added stress to his life in a variety of ways. By flirting with his female friend, he avoided any family stress. An extramarital emotional connection will many times illuminate what is missing in a marriage. The connection may serve as a catalyst, forcing us to address issues and make choices about our marriages that have needed attention.

I encouraged this gentleman to assert himself and address his resentments with his wife. He was amazed at how responsive she was to his concerns. He took responsibility for his feelings. She knew that things were not right, but needed to hear clearly from him regarding the urgency of the problem. She awakened and began to make changes that altered patterns in their relationship. She stepped out of the bubble. She was able to make changes that helped de-stress both of them at home. I regularly tell couples that come for counseling that I am not interested in "saving their marriage." Salvaging something sounds like it may belong in a junkyard. I am interested in reconfiguring relationships so that they are more fulfilling. This may mean changing the dynamics of a relationship to make it more meaningful. This process takes time. There are no quick fixes when it comes to dealing with issues of marital discord. It takes awareness, rational thinking, staying in the moment, working with conflict, and an end to denial.

The Value of Psychotropic Medications

As I have stated, stepping out of the bubble is not easy. Many times I believe that people need an aid in the form of psychotropic medication to assist them. There are those in the mental health/wellness field who are beginning to speak out against the use of antidepressant medication and other mood stabilizing drugs. One high profile cognitive-behavioral presenter recently claimed that there is no scientific evidence to support the connection between levels of serotonin in the brain and depression. Therefore he does not advocate the use of medication for anxiety and depression. My experience with psychotropic medication is that in specific situations it can be helpful to people and at times may be necessary for many patients. I believe in balance and moderation, and when medications may be useful as a tool in making therapy more effective, I recommend patients receive a psychiatric evaluation.

A large number of researchers believe that a combination of antidepressant medication and cognitive-behavioral therapy is the most effective treatment for many patients suffering from anxiety and depression. From my experience with clients, I believe that this theory is valid. I agree with the FDA that the efficacy of antidepressants, particularly in children, is still in need of exploration. But medication management in concert with therapy is effective. When medication is necessary, it can be helpful in assisting an individual toward emotional and behavioral change if it is combined with therapy.

It is not unusual for patients resist the notion of taking medication for depression or anxiety. They'll say something like, "I don't want to take anything that will alter my mind; I want to keep my personality." My response to some medication critics is, "Then why is it that you persist in drinking persistently; do you not see the irony here? You are willing to self-medicate in a way that exacerbates your symptoms, but refuse to consider medication that may assist you in your battle with depression." The obvious explanation is that for some clients, self-medicating with alcohol is habit-forming. Some clients are not willing to let go of their self-defeating need. Others skeptical of medication management have gotten caught up in the ideological implications of this issue. I am not aware of any medication that does not have some risk attached to its usage. The issue is, does the benefit of taking the medication outweigh the risks associated with it?

Therapy for Counselors

A therapist cannot get someone to step outside of the bubble and experience the light of day if the person insists on staying in hiding. However, how can a person be expected to take the risk of changing if the client's counselor is afraid of having his issues scrutinized? I am amazed at the number of counselors who have never experienced the counseling process for themselves. Thankfully, many educational institutions that educate therapists mandate counseling as a part of their training program. In my opinion, no therapist should be licensed without having experienced the counseling process as a client. How can a therapist identify with his clients if he has never sat in the other chair?

Beyond the issue of identification, many counselors *need* to be in the client chair. Are we to assume because of the role, a counselor has no emotional baggage to be explored? The issue of counselor burnout, transference, and counter transference is a significant one. No training program can assist a therapist with on-going problems with his own personal issues. Transference is the process whereby a client projects feelings onto the therapist. The feelings may be anger, mistrust, sexual feelings, or approval needs. Sometimes it is difficult for the therapist to maintain a sense of detachment from a client's projected feelings. Getting hooked by them may cause stress. Counter-transference is the process wherein the therapist identifies with the patient's problems in a way that is not helpful to the therapeutic alliance. The counselor may be suffering from issues similar to the patient and the counselor's feelings may infringe on the counseling process. The counselor may have a particular therapeutic bias and that perception may impede therapeutic progress. A counselor may also have unresolved issues that interfere with the counseling process. The client may sense this and terminate therapy for that reason.

However, those who conduct therapy do not need to have every issue resolved in their own life in order to be effective. The point is that those who are entrusted to help others need to be aware of potential ways that their biases, feelings, thoughts, and behaviors can influence others in a negative way. Counselors need to seek the support of colleagues, supervisors, or therapists when conflicts occur which affect the collaborative relationship with patients. Counselors have an ethical obligation to refer patients who they are uncomfortable in treating to other therapists. For example, those who are uncomfortable in dealing with sexual predators should waste no time in referring such a patient to a treatment facility or counselor who deals with this special client population.

Freed From the Contents of Consciousness

It was Roberto Assagioli, the great Italian psychiatrist, who used to suggest that we repeat to ourselves, "I am not my feelings, my feelings may be sad, irritated, and happy - I am not my thoughts, my thoughts may be clear, confused, or irrational - I am not my body, my body may be sore, weak, or energized - I am I, a centered, loving human being."

As a therapist, I must personally have separated my feelings of shame and fear from who I am. Like my clients I ask myself, from where do these feels originate? For me, the source is my childhood perceptions. I can remember on many occasions cringing at critical statements that my parents made about my attitude or behavior. They meant no harm, but I was a sensitive kid and took these words to heart. I felt embarrassed and ashamed. I was afraid of my parents rejecting comments. I felt like a bad little boy who had disappointed his parents. Now I am in a position to disengage from these feelings. I can quarantine them. Shame and fear don't have to have power over me. I am free to let go of feelings that have kept me locked in the bubble. I am not a victim and try to teach my clients that they are not either.

The Anxious Caretaker

Many times people who are anxious or depressed are chronic caretakers. Those who have a long-standing pattern of caretaking typically live a guarded life. I once had a patient who came to see me about his current relationship. He previously had been married and now was in a very volatile partnership. According to this client, his female partner was plagued by a mood disorder. His partner would rapid cycle from being nice and then would go on a tirade of verbal insults. She would call my patient abusive names. But his goal was to fix her. He loved her and felt that with some help on his part that she would reform. He had this image of the two of them living as a happy couple along with their two children from previous marriages.

During one session, he walked in and plopped down a book on my sofa about verbal abuse. "What are you doing with this book?" I asked. "I just wanted to know more about what makes my girlfriend respond the way she does," he replied. "I think it is commendable that you want to know more about her problem, but how do you feel that this is going to impact your relationship?" I asked. "Her moods cycle and I thought it would be helpful to learn more about her so we can move forward together." His girlfriend was clueless about his attending therapy, never once showed any interest in coming for counseling and never was evaluated for her disorder. Many people are addicted to the "manic" or intense aspects of a relationship. In fact, they may feel that a "normal" relationship is too boring for them. Although the downside of the relationship may be highly abusive and dysfunctional, many clients will dismiss that aspect of the relationship. This gentleman preferred to focus on the intense positive shared moments and believed that he had the power to affect all that was wrong with the partnership.

This was not a good prognosis for relationship happiness. But my client maintained his insistence on working on the relationship even though his partner had not shown any desire to change. He was afraid to look at his own issues- feelings of fear of abandonment, lack of self-confidence, lack of boundary setting, and lack of assertiveness.

Caretakers love to help others at the expense of their own personal development. They are dedicated individuals who are committed to others' well being. Although such a mission is noble, caretakers rarely focus on their own needs. It is more comfortable and soothing to take care of others, than to look at one's own issues. Many times I see women who have "gone on strike," fed up with the fatiguing role of serving the needs of everybody else in the family. They come to see me because they are tired of continuously helping others and feel a need to find personal empowerment. This may be the first time the caretaker has ever faced her own needs. This client may have learned in childhood the underlying assumption, "God first, family second, and me third."

When a therapist tries to explore with a caretaker his personal wants, desires, and needs, the caretaker invariably feels selfish. Those who foster the courage and choose to stay in therapy are able to "find themselves" for the first time. For mothers, leaving behind the caretaking role may be dangerous business, because family members may balk at the change. Mother is now setting limits, being assertive, and acting empowered with affirming thoughts about her needs and aspirations. She has given up the need to pay her undivided attention to other family members. They must fend for themselves.

Caretakers come to counseling because they have never taken the time for self-discovery. They have been so caught up in caring for others, that they dismiss their own needs. One of my clients who was a caretaker, actually lived at home until she was in her mid-twenties because her mother was unable to function well enough to take care of several younger siblings. The mother suffered from depression and consequently this young lady was thrust into a parenting role for her brothers and sisters. She handled a great deal of responsibility at a very young age and is now respected by her siblings for all that she did to make life manageable for them.

But caretaking can create problems. This young lady was in a relationship with a partner who was dependent. Her partner was clingy and very irresponsible. My client admitted that she had very little in common with her boyfriend, but she hung onto the relationship anyway. What underlying assumption did my client embrace that sustained the relationship? Her response was, "Life is about taking care of others at the expense of meeting my own needs." That was the pattern she learned during childhood.

She had no concept of a relationship based on mutual respect and affection. She had indicated that her boyfriend loves her, but she had no affectionate feelings about him at all. In fact, she had reiterated the fact that she resents his intrusions into her life. She recognized the need to leave the relationship, but hung on because that is what he wants. She has a history of comfort in caretaking for others and was unwilling to assert herself toward ending the involvement. She was afraid of meeting someone who might be her equal in terms of education, occupation, and interests. The fear of intimacy was a byproduct of a pattern of caretaking for others. Caretaking creates a false sense of comfort, and therefore the risk of loving is avoided.

Through counseling, this client must learn to recognize the codependent pattern, observe the negative consequences, and develop the confidence to let go and move on in her life. Since she has never explored her own needs, this process will take time. She must learn through our time together that she deserves better. Her needs, her wants must come first. A change in thinking will lead to personal empowerment and confidence.

The Pitfalls of External Validation

People who depend on others for affirmation are often anxious or depressed. Those who rely on inner validation from outside sources are doomed to feelings of emptiness. This holds true for women who think they can define themselves through a relationship with a man. Many women, due to the fear of abandonment, cling onto relationships that are unhealthy. Even when a woman is exposed to a great deal of abuse and manipulation, the relationship continues. The abuse creates self-doubt in the partner, and the pattern is sustained. "Maybe I am at fault," they respond, even after multiple abusive events. Ironically, self-doubt is what leads them into the relationship, and is also what serves to sustain the connection. I tell women that they need the kind of constructive anger (energy) that helps them to "get themselves back from others." It's the inner feeling and thinking which says, "I don't deserve to be treated this way - I'm not putting up with this anymore no matter how much I love him." Many of us are afraid to set limits and boundaries. We get caught up in our partner's perspective. "I can't set limits because what would he think? If he becomes upset with my boundaries, he might decide to leave me. God forbid that that should happen."

A single women client of mine met with me and shared a very interesting interaction. She and a date had gone back to her apartment to watch a movie. They had recently met, so there was no significant development in the relationship. While watching the movie, he reached over and proceeded to kiss her. She responded. He wanted to go further and made further sexual advances. She told him that she was not comfortable with doing more sexual play. Her response was, "What am I doing to you?" He reacted by saying, "You knew what I wanted and you're just being stubborn." She reacted by saying, "Get yourself out of my house, now!" This is boundary setting. From her perspective, "How dare he assume that I wanted to go "all the way." How dare he try to guilt me into doing something I'm not open to doing." That's the kind of energy that I wish people possessed. I teach my patient to honor their own perspective as being more important than all the clamoring voices around them. I was counseling a woman who recently went through a divorce. She never felt validated in her marriage and acceptance was based on the accomplishment of tasks that pleased her husband. In childhood, she never felt accepted or affirmed by her parents. Now she is in a relationship with a man who cherishes her. He accepts her inner beauty. He really knows her and values her for her character. She is amazed that anyone could love her the way her boyfriend does.

The downside for her is that the new relationship has illuminated all the fears, feelings of abandonment, and issues of self-worth that plague her. She struggled with her vulnerability because she has never been this transparent before. Rather than act on the urge to hide, I asked her to quarantine her mistrustful feelings. She must act as if they aren't there when she is with her friend. I suggested that she pull the feelings out of storage when she chooses to address them. Then I directed her to journal about her troublesome feelings until the ungrounded energy passes. Feelings just are. They have no power over us if we give them expression when we choose to deal with them. In our behavior, we need to detach from the feelings and act as if they are not a part of us.

For example, when she is with her boyfriend, she needs to communicate in a way that is grounded and needs to put her scary feelings aside. If she is unable to put her feelings aside, she needs to share them honestly with her partner. If she is afraid because he does not call her, she needs to get feedback from her partner and share her sense of discomfort. This is authentic communication.

V. REFLECTIONS ON THERAPEUTIC STRATEGIES

Much of an individual's pain may be existential in nature. One may possess feelings of aloneness, lack of meaning, lack of clearly defined goals and activities that can create symptoms of anxiety and depression. These are the people that need to reconfigure their life. Sometimes helping a patient "build a life" is more important than dealing directly with their irrational thoughts and behavior. When a client's needs are not being met, he may gravitate toward behaviors that are self-defeating. In such cases, dealing with the client's needs may be more important than focusing on the painful byproduct of passivity. In other words, change may minimize the psychic pain without directly managing the painful symptoms.

For example, I had a teenage client who was obsessing about his shame and fear because he felt compelled to look at pornography. He just couldn't get rid of the obsession. Since he was rather socially anxious, I worked with him on developing friendships at school. He was making progress in his friendship building, and he finally confided in me that he was fond of a girl at school. He had never dated before so this was quite a significant event. By focusing on this particular need, his obsessing lessened in severity. He had been sublimating his feelings through sexual material.

Many times obsessive thinking and behavior is tied to other situational factors. In this client's case, anxiety about socialization, particularly with the opposite sex was a significant precipitating issue. I felt that if I could direct my client toward a positive connection with a girl, his fantasy life would diminish in significance. During the next counseling session he was elated. He had dated the girl, they were maintaining contact, and he no longer felt consumed by his ritualistic thinking. If you encourage others toward meeting their needs, many irrational thoughts and behaviors will diminish in significance. At the onset of counseling, it took extreme courage for this youngster to share his troubling thoughts. But by doing this, he opened himself up to the possibility of letting go of his obsessions in favor of real life experience.

People who obsess have a tendency to flare, because they become frustrated when things don't go their way. Their perfectionism causes them to store anxiety until they reach the breaking point. I remember a friend telling me about his two year old son. His son would sit next to him on the floor. His son would have him take a piece of paper and fold it. Then he would ask him to fold it again. This pattern would be repeated until his father could no longer fold the paper. When the child realized that his father was finished folding, the toddler would have a temper tantrum, throwing himself on the floor kicking and screaming. Although the little boy has outgrown this behavior, many people who obsess continue to become frustrated when anything thwarts their ability to maintain their rituals.

Rational Responding to Anxiousness

Patients need to learn to rationally respond to problems rather than internalizing them if they are to find psychological healing. I always tell my patients that they are responsible *to* people not *for* them. The distinction is a significant one. Owning people's feelings is a painful process, and quite self-defeating. My mother occasionally will comment, "I worry about you!" I'm glad she cares about me, but it's as if people think that they can keep us out of harms way by agitating about our problems. Worrying is a useless habit. We think that we can ward off impending doom by being a worrier. We think that we are protecting others by being anxious for them. It is an exercise in futility.

I like to assist my clients in transitioning from worry to what Albert Ellis, the founder of *Rational-Emotive-Behavioral Therapy* calls appropriate concern. Appropriate concern involves developing a sense of necessary detachment from the problem. You are able to take a step back and get a sense of perspective. You are not emotionally swallowed-up by any issue. If you are appropriately concerned about challenges, you are in a position to break the issue down, problem-solve it, and take necessary action to correct the problem. Worriers get emotionally hooked and create self-defeating behaviors that block them from handling the problem. They have no resources to solve anything because they get caught up in a self-defeating, maladaptive cycle of thoughts and feelings.

People need to learn to respond in a rational manner. Rational responding is a process in which clients refute the nonsensical beliefs that they embrace. Rational responding involves talking to oneself in a way that is nurturing, reasonable and based on reasonable evidence. For example, an anorexic client may say that her current weight is just perfect. As a therapist, I may say," Let's check out the evidence for your assessment. I want you to survey five people and get their feedback on whether your current weight is about right for you." The anorexic individual will be reluctant to do the assignment because she knows what others think about her condition. So I might say, "One of the cardinal features of eating disorders is that the person's perception of their weight is distorted. Keeping that in mind, where's the evidence that your perception is more accurate than mine or others who would rate you as being too thin?"

This process of shifting responsibility to the disorder is called reattribution. It helps the client to realize that they are more than the nature of their disorder. The client can learn to distance herself from the disorder and develop confidence in one's "real" self. The real self or observer self is the part of us that can look at the contents of consciousness and realize that we are much more than what we see, feel, and think.

Staying in the Moment

Awareness involves staying in the moment. Not "looking in the rear view mirror"and not anticipating the future. Awareness means being mindful. Mindfulness is the Eastern concept for staying in present awareness. People who are mindful are able to empty themselves of the clutter of the past and future and stay focused on present experience. This is not easy. If you have ever tried meditation you know how difficult this process can be. That is why I recommend guided tapes to assist patients with moving towards a deeper state of relaxation and focus. Even with guided imagery, one's mind tends to wonder onto the clutter of consciousness. During meditation, when we drift, it is important that we don't get upset with ourselves but gently refocus our efforts passively toward the directives of the meditative guide.

Often I have my anxious clients practice mindfulness. Regrets over the past and anticipatory worries about the future are self-destructive. Staying in present awareness is a key to dealing with anxiety and depression. It is important to teach people to be more mindful. For example, when a patient takes a shower, I will direct him to be aware of the beads of water hitting his skin. I direct clients to feel and enjoy the experience of lathering their skin with soap, washing, and drying off. I'll ask them, "What do you typically think about while you are taking a shower?" Invariably, the answer turns to anticipatory thoughts about events happening during the day. Most cannot say that they remember the experience of showering because their mind is projecting into the future. I also ask people who drink tea or coffee to feel the warmth of the cup and to be aware of the sensation of warmth as the cup of drink reaches their mouth. This is mindfulness. Everything that is done in therapy takes hard work, and mindfulness is a skill that is learned through practice.

Mindfulness involves moving away from the contents of consciousness to the "observer self." The observer self is the part of us that can detach itself from the clutter of everyday living. It is the grounded part. It is authentic. It is the part that is not swayed by every inner voice that taps into our awareness. As I mentioned earlier, our inner voice must be more convincing than all the other voices that clamor for attention. Staying aware means that our inner voice is controlling our decisions. The aware ego is the grounded, rational voice within that knows how to affirm and comfort us as needed. It acts as our inner-parent that nurtures us when we need it the most. Our aware inner voice is much more expansive than our thoughts, feelings, and bodily sensations. It is much more than what we think, feel and believe about ourselves.

Rational Responding to Maladaptive Thinking

Staying grounded means treating oneself with respect and kindness. However, those who live in the bubble tend to stay trapped in the paralysis of self-blame. I always have people tell me the thinking behind their self-blame. As Karen Horney wrote many years ago, their statements are usually filled with the "tyranny of the shoulds." Albert Ellis calls this process *must-er-bation*. He believes that most neurotic behavior involves the erroneous assumption that we *must* be loved and valued by *all* the significant people in our lives or it would be horrible. Additionally, we *must* be able to control *all* the circumstances and events that affect our lives or it would be catastrophic and we *ought to* pay people back if they don't act they way we want. Ellis believes that moving our thinking toward *preferences* rather than *demanding* that things be the way we want them to be, frees us from irrational thinking. Moving my patients from internal maladaptive responses to more rational ways of thinking and behaving is a goal of therapy.

Sometimes I use Aaron Beck's *Daily Dysfunctional Thought Sheet* as a way of getting my patients to monitor thinking, feelings, and behavior. Beck is founder of the *Cognitive therapy* model of behavioral health treatment. By having people write out negative thinking and feelings associated with situations and events, I am able to help patients make a connection between faulty thinking and difficulties such as anxiety and depression. There is a column on the Daily Dysfunctional Thought Sheet that provides the client with an opportunity to list rational responses to negative automatic thoughts. For example, a patient may say, "I'm falling apart. I can't handle this situation." A rational response to such a maladaptive statement might be, "Sometimes I just feel overwhelmed. But I've handled things like this in the past. Just take it one step at a time and I will be fine." Rational responding can be an empowering process for clients.

Recognition is the first condition in stepping out of the bubble. The most difficult step is assisting clients in the process of responding more rationally to one's irrational inner dialogue. Speaking the truth about oneself is hard. Many of us have not had the nurturing or appropriate parenting to guide us in the process of self-affirmation. As Albert Ellis urges in *Rational-Emotive-Behavioral Therapy*, I try to direct people out of an inner dialogue filled with *musts* to softer inner responses filled with *preferences*. Responses such as, "It would be preferable if people acted the way I desire, but that is not necessary. I can tolerate it if people respond to me in stupid ways."

As Jeffrey Young, a Cognitive therapist suggests, I sometimes do a point-counter-point interaction with patients in order to assist clients in moving toward more rational thinking. I play the role of the irrational, maladaptive inner voice and give my clients the opportunity to role-play more rational ways of responding to events. This process helps to objectify that which is internal. My goal is to assist the client in moving toward more positive inner dialogue that is supportive.

Panic Disorder

Many individuals come to me because of extreme anxiety, usually with bouts of panic. People who live with panic experience symptoms such as chest tightness, shortness of breath, racing heart, and a need to isolate from people. Many have lived with the symptoms for a long time. Sometimes the panic is triggered by a traumatic experience. One client came to see me because of panic associated with a vehicle accident. She was a nurse assisting a patient in the back of an ambulance and was hit broadside by a truck. The accident left her with numerous injuries and triggered symptoms of fibromyalgia, depression and panic. After the accident, she was afraid to drive or ride in a vehicle. She was petrified when she would pass cross streets due to the hypervigilence caused by the accident. Hypervigilence is the startle response that typically affects people after enduring a traumatic event.

Working with client's who experience the fallout from anxiety, depression and panic is challenging. Since I typically use a cognitive-behavioral therapy approach, I start by assessing my client's thought patterns. This anxious client was easy to work with because most people who suffer from anxiety are highly compliant. She was compliant in completing any homework assignments. I had her focus on her secondary emotional symptoms, because those symptoms tend to keep the anxiety active. She would ruminate with thoughts like, "Oh my God, here it comes again!" There's that awful panic again; I can't breath, I'm going to suffocate, I'm surely going to die, my chest hurts, I must be having a heart attack." Accordingly, the sympathetic nervous system ramps-up in response to the irrational thinking and a full-blown anxiety attack ensues. Dealing with the secondary symptoms of panic, or the "panic over the panic" is the key to minimizing its affect on clients.

Posttraumatic Stress Disorder

Many people have experienced Posttraumatic Stress Disorder symptoms. One client was in a highly abusive relationship with a man who physically beat her. This went on for some time as she allowed herself to remain in a pattern to be re-traumatized. Currently, relationships still terrify her. Due to mistrustful thinking, she pushes men away with her anger and rage. Then she becomes upset with herself for behaving in impulsive ways. The key to treatment for her is to isolate the traumatic feelings, explore the pain around them, and to teach her new ways of behaving that are based on rational thinking. She no longer needs to view herself as the victim in relationships. She needs to expand her psychic map to include new feelings, thoughts, and behavior. This exploration process is painful, but it will free her of the need to continue victimizing herself. She needs to flush out the negative energy that has allowed her to be retraumatized. The cycle can be broken with proper therapeutic intervention.

Clients who suffer from Posttraumatic Stress Disorder experience the effects of psychic numbing. These people also tend to suffer from anxiety, depression, panic, anger and rage and startle response. A friend of mine, who was a Lieutenant during the Vietnam War, experiences features of this disorder. When the snowplows rumble

69

through his hometown during a major snowstorm, it is not unusual for him to be awakened in the early morning by the sounds. Sometimes he jumps out of bed in total confusion and panic. It's as if he is back in the rice paddies of Vietnam waiting for the next mortar round to explode. What he is experiencing is a startle response or hypervigilence. Isn't it amazing how the brain operates? After thirty years, loud noises still take him back to a place where psychic numbing was necessary for survival. All of the painful psychic energy is stored in our bodies and mind. Many times I recommend message therapy as an adjunct treatment to clients who have stored painful feelings, because it is one more entry point for ferreting out troublesome emotional energy.

Dealing with Secondary Anxiety Symptoms

The key to dealing with anxiety and panic is not in dealing with the primary symptoms, but in attacking the nonsensical things we tell ourselves about the anxiety. Everybody suffers from anxiety, but not everyone castastrophizes about it. For example, let's say you are taking a midterm exam in college. You open the test book and realize immediately that you are not familiar with some of the material and appropriate answers. You can respond in one of two ways: "Oh man, none of this looks familiar to me; I'll never get this, I'll never pass this test; if I don't pass this test I'll fail for the semester; My parents will just die if I flunk out of school." Or you can respond by thinking,

"Now just hold on a second, some of this material looks a little unfamiliar, but I'll just calm down and start working on the questions I do know. I can always go back later and tackle the more difficult ones." Anxiety itself is not the focus of therapy, rather it's the secondary thoughts that we keep telling ourselves about anxiety that paralyzes us. The secondary thoughts are the focus of treatment.

Aaron Beck, founder of Cognitive therapy, calls this the "downward arrow effect." We start out with anxiety and proceed to become disturbed about our anxiety that leads us further in a downward emotional spiral. Maladaptive thinking creates the conditions for the downward spiral. With my clients, I work on calming secondary fears. I also assist the client in dealing with defective thoughts about being a panicky person. Clients may assert, "I am a louse because I tend to panic at times."

I recall a time after my father died that I developed some panicky feelings. They were quite uncomfortable. One of the keys with dealing with panic is having an escape plan. If your thoughts and emotions get too difficult to handle, you can remove yourself from people and situations, if necessary. One day I had to make a presentation to a group of educators. I agitated about it for days. I was afraid I would not be able to perform effectively. I was afraid that panicky thoughts and feelings would prevent me from presenting appropriately. "What if I get up in front of all these people and forget what I need to say?" With a bit of humility, I decided to have a talk with my superior about my dilemma. "What would he think of me when I told him my story?" I notified him of my anxiety and asked him to be ready to fill in if I needed him. But after talking to him I realized that something significant had happened. By sharing my story of grief and panic, I became lighter. I felt freed from the burden of hiding my pain. My superior understood and would have done anything to help me. He *had* helped me by merely listening to my concern. Paradoxically, I felt free to give my talk.

Panic and Phobic Flyers

One of my specialties is working with phobic flyers. One of the things I try to stress is that panic is time-limited. You know that as bad as it feels, it will end within a brief time frame. Usually people who fly have the biggest problem during the first ten minutes of the flight. It's the boarding, waiting, speeding down the runway, and the ascent. I help flyers stay grounded during this period by coaching them to keep both feet on the floor, leaning back on their chair, securing proximity seating near the front of the plane, using head sets, and by having them secure prescribed mild anti-anxiety medication for the first run, if needed.

I used to take my clients to the airport prior to 9/11 and have a representative from the airlines meet us and take us on a plane early in the morning prior to a hectic day at the airport. The representative would explain the features of the plane, let the client into the cockpit, and review with my client the meticulous set of standards that pilots need to adhere to prior to clearance for takeoff. This activity frequently helped relieve some of the client's anxiety. In conjunction with therapy, I also use a program called *Help for the Fearful Flyer* by Captain T.W. Cummings, former pilot for Pan-American Airlines. The program is very educational, informative and helpful in assisting clients in managing their anxiety. I also recommend the reading of *The Joy of Flying: Overcoming the Fear* by retired TWA Captain W.H. Gunn. It is incredible to me that some airlines have no comprehensive program to assist phobic flyers. Wouldn't you think such a program would be deemed cost effective, particularly in today's airline industry?

There are ways for people to manage the fear of flying by:

- Dealing with anticipatory anxiety by means of cognitive rehearsal (mentally creating imagery of events surrounding the entire flight process).
- Learning how to relax during the takeoff. The first ten minutes of the flight, including the ascent are the most troublesome.
- Securing preferential seating arrangements, if possible.
- Learning how to manage passenger reactions to one's fear.
- Dealing with feelings of being trapped while flying.
- Refocusing attention on activities while flying which minimize fear and anxiety.

Embrace Your Symptoms

Sometimes I have individuals schedule a panic time. This technique is called paradoxical intention. This is a time when I encourage clients to feel the full impact of their panic. The irony of this method is that patients inform me that they have trouble bringing the panic on. The paradox is, that once we quit fighting with panic and anxiety, and actually embrace it, the effects tend to dissipate. I implore my patients to quit analyzing and ruminating over their panic and to respond more rationally to their panic episodes.

Since panic episodes are time-limited, I assist patients in learning to accept their feelings. When we fight with any part of ourselves, we are more likely to exacerbate the symptoms associated with the maladaptive patterns. I instruct people to resist the urge to rid themselves of their symptoms, because it only makes them worse. I encourage them to fight the urge to analyze symptoms, because it only intensifies the effect. Let your symptoms be what they are, with the attitude that, "I can handle this anxiety management stuff. If I relax into my panic using deep diaphragmic breathing, it will more quickly subside." Fighting pain makes pain more painful! Join hands with your symptoms and they will be less troublesome.

Brain Lock

Obsessive-compulsive behavior is like imbibing too much alcohol. It works as a short respite from psychic pain, but ultimately exacerbates the extent of our suffering. Obsessing about things is an example of neurotic suffering that keeps our "brain locked," according to Jeffrey Schwartz. Those who are obsessive-compulsive may have difficulty managing certain aspects of their life.

Although there's a genetic predisposition to Obsessive-Compulsive Disorder, many of my clients have been helped to deal with their problem through family systems and cognitive-behavioral therapy. Years ago I had a friend who had similar interests and we connected very well. When I would propose that we go out and do some activity together, he would be resistant. I was having trouble figuring out the problem. However, I had noticed that everyday during the summer he would mow his lawn. He would cut it in one direction and then proceed in another path.

I finally asked him about his ritual and he confessed that his obsession was consuming a significant amount of his time. When he was done grooming the outside of his house, he would start inside the house by vacuuming for hours. He was embarrassed by his obsessional behavior and it significantly restricted his social life. I felt saddened that we were not able to do more activities together. At that time, medications for OCD (Obsessive-Compulsive Disorder) were not as effective as the current antidepressant medications.

For many people, Obsessive-Compulsive Disorder responds well to a combination of antidepressant medication and cognitive-behavioral therapy. Most OCD patients appear to be predisposed to the symptoms. Usually you can find other family members who share a similar pattern of obsessive-compulsive behavior. Therapeutic treatment involves relabeling, reattribution, relaxation techniques and refocusing strategies.

- **Relabeling and reattribution techniques** are designed to assist the client in objectifying the disorder and realizing they are more than their obsessions. For example, I teach people to respond by saying, "A part of my brain works in ways that makes me repeat things continuously. This is merely my disorder speaking. I am more than my disorder."

- **Relaxation techniques** may involve exercise, music, message, meditation and vacationing in a soothing environment. These strategies slow down the sympathetic nervous system creating less anxiety and making it easier for people with OCD to manage their thoughts and behaviors.

- **Refocusing techniques** refer to assisting clients to shift from obsessional thinking and behavior to other more self-rewarding activities. This change in activities lessons the impact of the obsessional behavior. For example, a child may have a ritualistic pattern of continuously changing the television channel switcher in a certain order. My goal is to get the child to leave his obsession by getting up and leaving the room, possibly departing the house for a brief walk. I have people track the intensity of their anxiety during the time that they are away from their ritualistic behavior. When removed from an obsessional behavior, anxiety always initially becomes worse and then dissipates in strength over time. Once the child returns to the obsessional pattern after voluntarily leaving it, it usually has decreased in its impact and intensity. Many clients will say, "I was able to keep from repeating the pattern continuously. I only did it twice!" Reinforcement and encouragement are important for people attempting to minimize obsessive patterns.

Many adults are obsessive due to situational events such as traumatic experiences during childhood. Because much of an individual's childhood may have been unpredictable, obsessive-compulsive behavior is a mechanism for maintaining a sense of control over one's current environment. Sometimes, flushing out painful feelings resulting from childhood trauma assists clients in minimizing the effects of the OCD pattern. They are able to learn to feel more in control without relying on their disorder to maintain a sense of equilibrium.

Threads That Link Addictive Behavior

Many of us have features of an addictive personality. We heed the call to the "pleasure center," located in the frontal lobe of the brain. As many of us yield to the urges and cravings of the pleasure center, our negative beliefs and behaviors reinforce the need to continue self-defeating addictive behavior. Beneath the addiction, one finds personality characteristics which sustain the addiction. According to Charlie Whitfield, an author on addictive behavior, these characteristics are common to all addictions. People most likely experience problems with trust, dependency, abandonment, shame, guilt and the expression of deep feelings. Once the addiction is uncovered, these issues must be addressed through group addiction meetings or individual therapy.

Often, adults whose parents were alcoholics, choose to attend Adult Children of Alcoholics meetings in order to resolve the fallout from family behavior. Family members can be affected by addictive behavior and may adopt behavioral characteristics similar to the addict.

Addictive behavior lies on a continuum. For some of us, our tendency to compulsively engage in a particular behavior may not affect our everyday functioning. For example, many people engage in a pattern of ritualistic jogging. This may be considered a positive addiction because the activity promotes physical fitness and can release endorphins that elevate one's mood and behavior. If, however, the jogger begins to dismiss friendships, social activities and responsibilities in order to sustain the jogging pattern, then the activity takes on a different meaning. Furthermore, many joggers may become so obsessive about their interest that they begin experiencing significant weight loss, making them appear too thin and fostering body misperception problems.

Many people struggle with addictive patterns such as weight loss, gambling, sexual addictions, eating disorders, compulsive shopping and self-cutting. I am merely providing a brief list of addictive behaviors. A comprehensive list is too exhaustive to print.

Many people ask me, "Are there any common characteristics or features that link various addictions into a pattern?" The following is my perception of the common threads that link all addictive behaviors:

- Most addictive behaviors are an attempt at avoiding unpleasant and painful experiences.
- Most addictive urges and underlying self-defeating beliefs trigger cravings.
- Most people with addictions experience masked emotional problems such as anxiety, depression and obsessive-compulsive characteristics.
- Most addictions are fueled by thwarted anger and self-blame, particularly among adolescents.
- Shame-based beliefs and feelings are at the core of all addictions.
- Most of us who experience addictions complete a "repetition cycle" of abuse. The cycle starts with an

experience or urge, yielding to the cravings, feeling numb with a decrease in anxiety, manifesting guilt and remorse, followed by an escalation of anxiety and a repeat of the cycle.

- The primary goal of addictive behavior is to decrease anxiety.

Those of us who struggle with addictions would be well served to listen to a partner, a friend or one's own inner voice. People need to demonstrate courage by addressing their problem now, rather than waiting to "hit rock bottom."

Cognitive therapy and Mood Disorders

In addition to working with patients with anxiety disorders and addictive behavior, I also see those who suffer from mood disorders. Chronic depression, Major Depression, and Bipolar Disorder are the most common problems. Chronic depression is called Dysthymic Disorder. These people have experienced symptoms of depression for many years. Although the condition is more long-term and chronic than Major Depression, it is less severe in its symptoms. I compare it to a "low-grade fever" as opposed to the "severe flu" symptoms of Major Depression. Bipolar Disorder can take many forms but always involves cycling from an elevated, manic mood state to a depressive one. This cycling or mood shift process can take days, weeks, or sometimes hours. Like all mood disorders, it can be quite debilitating.

Many times, psychotic features are associated with those suffering from Bipolar Disorder. This may involve delusional or hallucinatory thinking and behavior.

People who are depressed have numbed out to the expansiveness of appropriate emotion. Depression and Bipolar Disorder can have associated symptoms of anxiety, sadness, interrupted sleep, impulsive behavior, eating irregularities, agitation, raging, loss of confidence, and a sense of hopelessness. Most clients feel trapped, lack motivation, display depleted energy, and have a sense of profound sadness. They feel helpless and extremely vulnerable. Nothing in life appears to bring them a sense of fulfillment and joy. At this time, Cognitive therapy in conjunction with antidepressant medication and/or mood stabilizers appears to be the most effective treatment.

In my practice, I work with depressive client's maladaptive automatic thoughts, cognitive distortions, and underlying beliefs.

- Automatic thoughts are spontaneous, as their name suggests, and can be quite self-defeating. Thoughts such as, "It would be awful if Sue turned me down for that date," is an example.

- A cognitive distortion represents the manner in which we process information. The automatic thought characterized above is the client's way of magnifying the severity of a situation. Magnification of circumstances and events is a type of cognitive distortion. When we

81

look out of our distorted lenses of reality, we invariably will suffer from personalizing, making inaccurate assumptions, discounting the positive and dwelling on the negative. For example, a person might say, "Girls *always* think I am socially crippled."

• The underlying belief with the client mentioned above might be, "Rejection is a horrible thing because I will feel abandoned." Helping clients test the validity of their underlying beliefs is a goal of cognitive-behavioral therapy. I might say, "Where is the evidence that rejection must be so horrible that you must feel rejected if Sue doesn't date you? Are their any other conclusions you can draw?" Helping clients with mood disorders deal more adaptively with their thoughts and behavior is essential to better functioning.

One of the key features held by people who are depressed is their sense of hopelessness. Many are unable to look beyond their immediate problem and see any options that would benefit them. I had worked with a woman who was involved in a troubled marriage. Her husband used power and control and bouts of anger to intimidate her. She did everything possible to keep peace at home for the sake of the children. She felt trapped, was resentful and regretted having married her husband.

Regardless of whether she stays in the marriage or not, my job was to assist her in building confidence. I needed to help her set personal boundaries, recognize ways in which she can change her life, and find activities apart from her husband that will bring her satisfaction and meaning. I needed to help her to assert herself with her husband by learning to respond more rationally and confidently in his presence. I needed to assist her in not getting caught up in the burden of her husband's feelings. She needed to learn to detach from counterreactions that her husband may display as a result of her new way of responding to him. Counterreactions are manipulative tactics that a partner may use when the dynamics of a relationship changes. Such strategies include using guilt, bullying, and creating self-doubt. She needed to ignore the counterreactions and recognize that she *does* have options that she can exercise that are in her best interest.

Acting As If

"Acting as if" is a behavioral strategy that works quite effectively in dealing with maladaptive thoughts and feelings. It is particularly important for depressive clients. Many depressed people view the future through the lenses of their depression. Getting clients to make even small changes in behavior can be difficult. If patients can learn to break an activity down, and move forward in accomplishing small tasks, more positive feelings will follow. The behavior change must precede the change in feelings. "Act as if" you can unpack that box and go ahead and do it. "Act as if" you can attend that social function and you will. Self-appraisal can come later. It is imperative that the therapist attempt to move his client in the direction of behavioral change. With depressed patients, doing must precede feeling.

Years ago I saw an individual who was referred to me by a psychiatrist. This man had mistrustful feelings. He was enraged at his wife because he thought she was having an affair with a former friend. Since "the other man" traveled a great deal, he envisioned this gentleman coming to her hometown and meeting up with his wife. When he first came to see me, he shared with me elaborate schemes that he conducted to try to catch the two of them together. However, none of the evidence established a connection between his wife and this man. I was suspicious of his "evidence". With that in mind, I met with the wife. She saw it as nothing more than a fabrication based on her husband's emotional issues of mistrust. She was very forthright and indicated she had no contact with this man that her husband was agonizing over.

At home my client would move into an emotional place of insecurity and paranoid feelings. He would lash out at his wife regarding her supposed affair. His wife tried to deflect her husband's insinuations, but many battles were fought over this issue. Finally I was able to get both of them into counseling to deal with their conflict. In joint counseling he continued to insinuate that his wife was having the affair. She would distance herself and accuse him of unnecessary mistrust. They were doing this chronic self-defeating dance. During one of our conjoint sessions, I was able to get my client to focus on his mistrustfulness apart from its connection to his wife. We explored his childhood and relationships with his parents, finding much fodder for discussion. Things were so dysfunctional in his family life that he felt rejection, humiliation, and abandonment. We were able to link his family history to his current feelings of mistrust and we began to make headway.

Often, he would come into counseling with his wife, begin to attack her verbally about her affair, and then I would start my therapeutic intervention by stopping him. I would assist him in focusing on his feelings of mistrust, rather than making her the focus of therapy. I requested that he "act as if" his wife was innocent of marital indiscretion while isolating his paranoid feelings. "Sometimes our feelings trick us into believing things that are not true; it's just possible that that may be happening here; you don't always need to act on your feelings until you know what they are telling you." Feelings just are. Sometimes you can trust what they tell you and sometimes you can't. But they will usually lead one to the source of an issue if patience is demonstrated. One day my client called me by phone and asked, "Are you sure my wife is being truthful?" "Yes," I said, "things are just fine; you need to quarantine your feelings for now until we can check them out; don't take them out on your wife; let's work on them together."

My client's feelings needed to be quarantined until we could explore them in a way where they would do no damage. Sometimes we can't step outside the bubble without help. We need others, maybe professional counselors, to assist us in exploring our thoughts and feelings to help us to make sense out of them. Emotional reasoning, the kind of distortion that says, "I feel like a dud, therefore I must be one" needs to be addressed in order to get one to recognize that feelings don't always represent the truth about whatever is troubling us. The more we explore our feelings without making value judgments about them, the less power they have to affect us in negative ways.

There Are No Gurus

Many times an individual will come into the counseling process with the notion that the therapist has a "bag of tricks" that he can use to cure them. The patient may view the therapist as the guru who has all of the answers. Such clients may play a passive role in the counseling process, waiting for the therapist to perform his magic. Little do these people know that they are deceiving themselves when they enter into counseling with these expectations. Within the counseling process, they may complain incessantly about physical symptoms, feeling confused, lacking the ability to crawl out of the hole they have made, or feeling utterly helpless. As I mentioned earlier, Fritz Perls used to say, it is my job to "frustrate the client appropriately." This means that I acknowledge my client's impasse but encourage him to find a way out of his problems with my guidance. Self-regulation is a goal of therapy. I educate people in the fact that all the answers are ultimately within. I am only there to help point people in the direction of recognition and self-empowerment.

Many clients will terminate counseling because I am not able to give them immediate advice that would break the impasse that they are experiencing. Losing these patients is unfortunate, because they need to stay and collaboratively work with me on a treatment plan. Unfortunately, many clients come for one visit only, hoping for a quick fix. I never see them again, and I wonder what happened to them. Usually, I will send a follow-up letter or make a phone call, but rarely do such people return.

Counseling is hard work for an individual, and I am certainly proactive with my clients, but I cannot do the work alone. I always tell parents to never do for your child what he can do for himself. This motto carries over to the counseling process. Effective counseling calls for collaboration between the therapist and client. Goals must be established with the guidance of the counselor and the patient must be committed to working on them. Homework assignments for patients are an important ingredient to successful therapy.

VI. REFLECTIONS ON BELIEF, FAITH, THINKING AND INJUSTICE

In order for one to be fully functioning, there must be a balance between the psychological and spiritual dimension of one's life. Everything must be open to consciousness. The more we make conscious, the more we realize there is a great deal that we do not know. Why do psychotropic medications work? Why do tear ducts work when we cry? How do we explain the complexity of the human body? It takes courage and integrity to say that our knowledge is limited. There are many things in the realm of psychology and spirituality that defy an answer or explanation.

Sometimes we don't have the perfect answer for us. I think that intellectually honest people will tell you that the more they learn, the more they feel limited by their knowledge base. In those cases we have to feel secure enough to say, "I'm not sure about that, let me give it some thought." If there's a religious issue we are struggling with, we have to feel confident enough to say, "I believe this to be true, but I don't know for sure if it's accurate." Intellectual honesty takes significant courage.

The Basis of Our Beliefs

Many clients belief system is a by-product of a foundation of poor parenting. If an individual has been exposed to ineffective parenting, a religious belief system may be based upon deficiencies in psychological development. Some client's believe in a "tyrant God," one who spreads gloom and doom. These patients will talk incessantly about how they have disappointed God, how they may have lost their salvation, and the guilt feelings they experience. They live with the fear that God is mad at them. Until one deals with problems related to psychological development, one's vision of religion and faith is distorted. People look out of the lenses of their depression, anxiety, and fear and make faulty interpretations about the nature of life and spiritual reality.

With change comes a certain period of disorientation. But if one can tolerate the groan zone, a client may move into a newer, fuller, richer place within. It is a place where we feel grounded, at peace with ourselves. There is a sense of humility that emanates from us as we view the world with wonder. We may sense that a higher power is working within us. We are not afraid of those who disagree with us. We are also not afraid to look at a variety of issues from a myriad of perspectives.

For example, if you are pro-life, can you build an argument to support the right to pro-choice? Some would suggest this way of thinking is preposterous. On the contrary, I believe that it is the only way to solidify what beliefs are really true for us. One must think multidimensionally in order to develop a strong conviction on any issue. A good debater or an excellent attorney always gathers information regarding an opponent's strongest argument. This in turn makes a case more compelling.

Multidimensional Thinking

In his book, *The Different Drum*, M. Scott Peck talks about the need for multidimensional thinking. A sense of community cannot exist without the richness of varying opinions and values. Looking at issues from different perspectives is what honest thinking and discourse is all about. But many would prefer to believe in their "belief" because it creates an image of safety. Being able to think about an issue from different viewpoints may create some inner tension, but it is a more honest means of reflecting. It demonstrates more integrity. It leads to stimulating discourse. Those who view issues from different perspectives may be considered by some to be indecisive. On the contrary, one cannot have strong, well thought out convictions without the ability to see multiple viewpoints.

I believe that people who think one-dimensionally lack depth. They are afraid to think outside their preconceived notions. Those who believe that there is a right way to view every problem are one-dimensional thinkers. These are the people who see no ambiguity, no shades of gray, nothing paradoxical. Such rigidity makes one feel safe in an insecure world. Sometimes these are the religious people whose rigid set of beliefs sustains them.

Theologian James Fowler alludes to this issue in his significant work, *Stages of Faith.* Fowler views belief and faith as polar perspectives. Belief is defined as a preconceived notion about the nature of one's worldview. Faith, however, is an unreserved opening to the truth wherever that process may lead. It is an opening to "knowing" through experience. It transcends religious dogma. Stepping out of the bubble involves faith, and faith demands that we sometimes move into the unknown of experience. This can be scary, but how wondrous at the same time. Dogma is not sufficient. It takes faith to move us into the growth zone.

One of my favorite verses in the Bible is where Jesus proclaims, "You seek the scriptures, for in them you think that you have eternal life, but they are that which testify of me." I believe he meant, "It's the spirit of who I am and what I say, not the letter of the law that counts." I believe that this statement speaks directly to those who operate out of spiritual tunnel vision rather than transcending religious dogma to the truth of one's experience. An example is the father who is a fundamentalist Christian who has believed all of his life that homosexuality is an abomination to God. During early adulthood, one of his children gathers the courage to come out and tell this father that he is gay. How does this father reconcile his beliefs with the nature of what his son has told him about his sexual orientation? This is a difficult spiritual and emotional dilemma. The father has several options to consider in making a decision on how to view this news. Do

I disown my own child for revealing his sexual identity? Do I admonish him to repent of his sins? Do I take the position of hating the sin, but loving the sinner? Or do I choose to let go of my need to reconcile my son's identity with my religious beliefs, and try to enlarge my spiritual map to include the possibility that God's grace may transcend the scope of my conflict? Enlarging our spiritual map is always a forward moving road. This is where we find the growth zone.

As I stated previously, the wiser and older we become, the more things we don't know for sure. M. Scott Peck makes this point in his various literary works. Part of intellectual honesty is admitting when you are uncertain as to the nature of phenomenon. Why do two people who were raised in the same environment play their lives out in dramatically different ways? How can those who have been seriously emotionally wounded as children turn out to be responsible, loving adults? The answer to these questions is perplexing. It is helpful to believe that some aspects of life are a mystery and we should honor that truth.

Religion at its Worst

Religious and spiritual expression can either bind people or free them of the shackles that have haunted them. Some time ago a woman called me looking for a therapist. She wanted a Christian therapist. I indicated that I would be more than willing to see her, and if she had spiritual concerns I would be open to addressing them. After several minutes of investigation on her part, she asked, "Do you go to church every Sunday?" I did not meet that criteria and therefore did not meet the litmus test of a good Christian counselor. One recent client who saw me for counseling proceeded with a litany of complaints about her husband, including verbal abuse, mood swings, and enduring her husband's extramarital connection with another woman. She was fed up with him and had decided to seek legal advice for a divorce. The following week she abruptly called me and cancelled our appointment because her husband had found a good "biblical counselor" for both of them to see.

This is religion as its worst. This has nothing to do with spiritual growth and commitment. It has more to do with a strict adherence to rules and beliefs that have been internalized without much thought. Many people would rather cling safely to the religious bubble, than to give creative thought to spiritual issues.

A young girl, who I have worked with in counseling, decided she needed some help with her religious thinking. This was a courageous step, since there is no room for wondering in her religious denomination. There was no room for doubt in her religion, and this adolescent had plenty of it. Authentic spiritual development leaves room for questioning. In fact, questioning aspects of one's faith tradition is a necessary ingredient to spiritual growth and development. Curiosity and doubt are preconditions to moving to a more mature level of faith development. Adolescence is a transitional period for such development. Most children can no longer internalize their parent's religious beliefs without some honest exploration of their faith. They must develop spiritual insights on their own. This process is a part of growing up. This is what separation and individuation are all about. That is, grappling with difficult spiritual issues and coming to a conclusion about what appears true.

Beliefs vs. Faith

People who have an underdeveloped faith system feel the need to adhere to strict guidelines and dogma to maintain a sense of security. They never venture out to question or challenge beliefs that have been passed down to them. They unreservedly believe certain ideas even though they may be in conflict with their knowledge or experience. Many of my clients have been told by church leadership that there is an easy answer for every problem. It would be nice if answers to complex issues came in a simplistic format, but they don't. People who believe simplistically are ultimately disillusioned because the perfect answer is not forthcoming. Guilt and disappointment follow.

Many people believe you must have an answer for every religious dilemma. That takes the mystery out of it! I tell my patients who question certain religious beliefs to say something like, "I believe this idea to be true, but I don't know for sure." Sometimes we are unable to reconcile our beliefs with reality. Our beliefs imply one thing and our experience tells us something else. Learning to live with spiritual ambiguity is necessary if we are to step out of the bubble. Rather than live with the tension created by living with ambiguity and paradox, some of us try to fit our conflicting reality into our system of beliefs. One may feel safer protecting our beliefs from reality, but it is not healthy and honest. This attempt at reconciliation leads to more conflict and confusion. We may even become angry, retorting, "Why do I see things so differently than the way I was taught to believe; I feel duped."

Living with Injustice and Grief

Living with paradox, ambiguity, and polarities is a necessary function if we are to stay reality-based. Staying conscious of things is a difficult experience. We must hold everything in tension. Clients sometimes complain in jesting that they wish they could go back to the days when their thinking appeared so simplistic! But there's no going back. Once you step over the line that takes you out the bubble, you can try to go back, but you can't stay in hiding for long. As John Dean exclaimed during the Watergate hearings, "You can squeeze the toothpaste out of the tube, but you can't get it back in again." Once things are made conscious, you can't go back on them. One must live with all the struggles that go with facing our experience without distorting it.

Everybody has a life story. Some of it is good and some of it is difficult and painful. Our stories are what make us human. Our stories are continually unfolding as we experience life outside the bubble. Many of us have struggled with deep wounding left over from childhood, failed relationships and the trauma of injustice. Stepping out of the bubble involves moving into the wilderness of experience and recognizing that we will come out of it renewed. This process calls for coming to grips with the full emotional impact of reality. When we explore this pain, we sometimes feel like we are capsizing. Some have asked me if they are going crazy. I encourage them by saying, "You are not going crazy, you are having crazy feelings; you can't go crazy from where you are; crazy people don't know that they have a problem."

Injustice is one of the most difficult life experiences to deal with. The death of a child, the loss of a job, being falsely accused of a misdeed, and discrimination are examples. Injustice can lead us to despise our accusers, to feel betrayed by those we thought we could trust to support us. Trying to face injustice is difficult but necessary. It is important to remember that we derive meaning out of doing the right thing, the loving thing, not catering to the needs of others. Others may disapprove of us for the decisions we make, but we do what we do for our own benefit and the benefit of those we serve.

A gentleman came to see me for counseling. His stature was intimidating. In a quiet voice he said to me, "What I'm about to say to you is going to make you think I'm weird." After assuring him that I have heard it all, he told me his story. "You see, I'm single and I lost my cat. My cat ran away and I haven't seen him for four weeks. I can't sleep at night and people are worried about me at work; I'm usually very upbeat, but not lately. I go to the kennel everyday in hopes that my cat will show up, but she hasn't yet."

We talked about holding on, letting go, grieving, and the images we all experience about things being different than they way they are. "How many times do I go to the kennel before I give up?" he exclaimed. What an interesting question. Stepping out of the bubble means letting go of the past and moving forward. My client can only answer that question for himself. He would prefer that I "gaze into my crystal ball" and provide him with an answer.

At some point, however, he will probably have to demonstrate the courage to let go of his cat and move on. This process will not be accomplished without many tears and feelings of anguish. But being in the here and now requires such courage. This gentle, but towering man will eventually face the truth, and realize that every disappointment can be redeemed. A new venture, a new life lies on the other side of his grief.

Some of the saddest stories, those of injustice, are the ones that relate to the treatment of children. I now have a better understanding as to why very few therapists and psychiatrists choose to practice with children. The price of the potential conflict in getting entangled in the legality of custodial issues makes providers of mental health services shy away from working with children. How sad, and yet the reality is that many states, including mine, have a horrific record when it comes to the issue of child advocacy and care.

Although many children are resilient, they may feel trapped by the ravages of divorce. Long term emotional scarring of children can be avoided if divorced parents work to rebuild their relationship with their children.

At times parents tell me that they have decided to stay in an unhealthy marriage relationship for the sake of the kids. For the most part, I am not impressed. Obviously, parents should make every effort, including involvement in marital counseling, before deciding to call it quits. Many circumstances, however, may dictate that it is in the best interest of the children to end the marriage. In the case of divorce, both parents must take responsibility for their marital shortcomings, learn to forgive themselves for their failure, and grieve the loss of the relationship. Most importantly, they must commit themselves to protecting their children from the emotional fallout of divorce.

Divorced parents, caught up in their own anger, sadness and grief, tend to project their feelings onto their children and former partner. As a result, children may experience a conflict of loyalties. After the divorce, parents need to work on rebuilding their relationship with their children. The following are some guidelines of what and what not to do:

- Both parents must be committed to staying involved in meeting their children's needs.

- Both parents must support each other in the process of parenting their children. Children feel more secure when parents work to maintain similar behavioral structure and limits.

- Both parents must refrain from making demeaning comments about the other parent, especially in front of the children. Many parents appear to have little insight into how such comments affect their children and how such verbal assaults will affect their relationship with their children over time.

- Both parents must refrain from using their children as "surrogate parents." By acting needy and victimized, parents hook their children into a care-taking role. Children will process this pattern and learn to resent it.

- Both parents need to resist the urge to over-parent. Divorced parents, motivated by guilt and fear of disapproval, may inadvertently create a codependent relationship by trying to be their best friend and overcompensating through permissive parenting and excessive spending.

- Both parents need to stay involved in the children's activities. Children want to see both parents at soccer games, school performances, karate lessons, and other events.

- Both parents need to establish a structured visitation process so that their children feel secure and clearly know what to expect in terms of household transitions.

Unfortunately, a divorced parent may refuse to "let go of the marriage" and fail to follow the advice that I have mentioned. In such cases, hopefully there will be one parent who transcends the divorce and is committed to the well-being of his children. As the Bible suggests, "You reap what you sow." Parents who emotionally refuse to let go of their partner and refuse to work collaboratively on behalf of their children, may end up doing irreparable harm to their kids. Those parent's who demonstrate integrity, by putting the needs of their children before their own, are more likely to build a positive, loving relationship with their children after the "dust of the divorce" has settled.

We need more providers who are willing to take the risks involved in practicing on behalf of our children, even in a highly litigious society. Those practitioners who have contact with juvenile court can attest to the misinformed, destructive decisions that are made on behalf of children. Some of the visitation decisions that are made by judges place a significant burden on our children. Court mediators make decisions that affect children without really listening and truly considering children's perspective about choices that impact their lives.

Some cases do protect the interests of children. I have been counseling a ten year-old child for over a year. Documents I received from the mother indicated that the father had supposedly abused my client. Also, several reports by police departments had been completed substantiating abuse. Numerous abuse reports had been submitted to Child Protective Services. The mother was frustrated because no one seemed to be interested in protecting this child from on-going emotional abuse by her father. As per the court visitation plan, this child was to spend part of the summer with her father. She went as she was directed to do and expressed to me that she was bored and lonely. There was no stimulation of interaction with other kids or adults during his summer visitation. According to the child, her father was verbally intimidating to her. She regressed during our counseling sessions and refused to discuss her feelings about the summer visitation. She began to get more hyperactive, displayed nervousness, and was guarded in her communication with me. All of this was out of character for this child. I sensed that she felt obligated to protect her father, even though things were not working out. It is not unusual for a child to protect an abusive parent out of loyalty.

Finally, the tension was too much and she unraveled in a conversation with her mother. She began telling her mother how bad things were with her father. During the next counseling session the child began telling me the truth about the ongoing yelling, screaming, and punishing demeanor of her father. She was terrified. She was also afraid that I would break confidentiality and tell her father how she really felt. Since there was a pending court deposition, the judge representing the case ordered that I turn over my records.

I turned the records over to my attorney who presented them to the judge. Several days later the judge called me and asked for my recommendations. I could not give recommendations due to issues involving my role, but told the judge that the records would tell the story. The judge decided to pull visitation access to the father until further notice. The mother was shocked that her child had been heard. The child was so relieved that she cried in the arms of her mother the night after the hearing. The mother was elated that the judge took the time to make a decision honoring a child's feelings by contacting me and asking for my opinion on the case. It appears that there are some legal experts who really do believe in child's rights. I will always protect the rights of children no matter how difficult the situation may be.

My impression was that child rights are not valued in many states and that the legal system works to the detriment of their wants, needs, safety and welfare. We live in a litigious society. Custodial cases are very delicate and present possible pitfalls for family members and counselors.

There are other stories of injustice that clients bring to counseling. People lose their cats, their marriage, their children, and their jobs. They feel the pain and anguish that accompanies such traumatic events. Do things happen for a reason? I don't think so.

Does it make any sense that we lose a child for a reason? As Rabbi Harold Kushner eloquently articulates in his book, *Why Bad Things Happen to Good People*, God is impartial.

At times we all suffer from the randomness of life and its consequences. The real question is, "How will I respond and redeem this experience? What will I learn and convey to others that will bring some meaning to this injustice?" Life isn't fair, and most of us have had a big enough dose of injustice to understand that. The problem is, we just don't want to face the pain and disappointment that accompanies the fact that life has hurt us. However, if we are to grow and move on, we must face the full impact of reality. We must not retreat, but stay out of the bubble and deal with what life delivers to us.

VII. REFLECTIONS ON KIDS AND PARENTING

Facing reality is sometimes very difficult. For teenagers it is highly troublesome. Kids are faced with a multitude of problems, such as coping with parents, dealing with age-mates, stressors at school, and dealing with various temptations. Youngsters have a variety of techniques for soothing their psychic pain without actually leaving the bubble. Self-cutting is one of the methods that some teens use to ward off emotional pain. They tell me that self-cutting actually temporarily blocks painful emotional issues. It serves as a misguided means of displacing troublesome emotions. In my opinion, most self-cutting is a result of thwarted anger. Youngsters who can't or are not permitted to express their feelings at home may use this technique as a part of their arsenal. Self-cutting numbs the pain for a brief period of time, but long-range frustration and resentment remains.

By teaching teens to project their anger outward rather than inward, the cycle can be broken. Teens also use various drugs, including alcohol, as a way of coping with psychological pain. The use of alcohol, marijuana, stimulants, muscle relaxants, and cough suppressants are popular substances. All of these substances are designed to provide the teen with a way to avoid life's struggles. These stimulants and depressants act as immediate gratifiers for pain. Drugs work on the "pleasure" center of the brain and blunt emotional trauma.

This fact makes self-medicating appealing to many, including youngsters.

I counseled a young girl who had a troublesome addiction. She was a charming teenager. She and I had an affinity right away and we quickly developed a positive counseling connection. But this young lady had a major problem. She was addicted to stimulant medication. In large doses she would experience hallucinogenic effects, become extremely disoriented, and stay awake for many nights. When she came to see me, she had already been hospitalized several times for this addiction. She attended Narcotics Anonymous for her addiction and had a personal sponsor.

During our sessions, she would make reference to the fact that her friends did not understand her addiction. As we progressed in our process, I was able to get a sense of the emptiness and fear that was behind her addiction. She was afraid of both success and failure. She tried to hold down a job but would end up sabotaging it. She tried to attend college classes, but would drop out due to a lack of motivation and a fear of failure. She would start the classes that were below her level of performance, and end up dropping out before the end of the semester making excuse for her inability to complete the courses. Then she would get into self-blame, ruminate and start the cycle of addictive behavior once again.

She could not grasp a vision of completing school and moving on into the workforce. She viewed her condition as hopeless although we discussed ways of building success, setting appropriate goals, self-affirmation, watching for triggers for using, and relapse-prevention strategies. She relapsed and ended up in an inpatient treatment center. I went to visit her and she seemed to appreciate the gesture. She was eventually released and returned to live with her parents. She came back to counseling and when she did she began opening up about her family. She perceived her older sister as a tyrant who continuously upset things at home. This was a pattern throughout childhood.

She began to withdraw from responsibilities at school and part-time work. She decided to move out of her parent's home and moved in with a girlfriend who had leased an apartment. We talked at length about the pitfalls of making this change. The girlfriend was a substance abuser and this scenario was not good. She did not do well with unstructured time and I saw this change as troublesome. But my client made the move anyway and I did not hear from her for several weeks.

Finally, I received a letter from her parents. The parents shared with great sadness how their daughter had died of heart failure due to complications from the drugs. Every imaginable thought raced through my mind. "What could I have done differently? How could such a pleasant young lady take her life?" I thought a great deal about how I would have felt if this young lady was my own daughter. I felt that I had done everything I could have done to assist her in dealing with her addiction. Fortunately, the parents felt the same way and never faulted me for my efforts.

Addictions can be nasty. And this one was disastrous. This young woman went back into the bubble for the final time. She couldn't muster the courage to face life the way it was. For whatever reason, life was too difficult for her. She couldn't handle the responsibility that was connected with every day living. She had learned to cop out when things got tough. Her fear had tripped her up and she had succumbed to it. I grieved the fact that she would never step out of the bubble and be the young woman that I envisioned her to be. There are many similar situations happening with kids every day and it is so sad because they have let themselves down, as well as the families and friends that will grieve their loss.

School Performance and Family Systems Issues

It is not uncommon for teenagers to use poor performance in school as a payback for unexpressed anger directed toward a parent. Several years ago I was seeing a teenager who was very bright. She was also failing numerous courses in middle school. Her parents brought her to counseling in the hopes that I could motivate her to try harder in school. After meeting with the parents, it became apparent that the mother and father were overfunctioning on behalf of this child. They would lecture, plead, contact the school, and set consequences trying to change the pattern of school failure. The child's father was away from home a great deal due to work, and when this dad was home he would lecture his daughter about the value of school.

107

Many times family systems problems are at the core of a teenager's difficulties. The child's behavior may be a metaphor for what is happening in the family. Parents may try too hard and paradoxically end up creating a power-struggle that promotes a major roadblock to academic success. This child mentioned above was angry with her father. When I approached her about using her grades as a wedge against her father, she admitted that she might be paying her father back. Her perception was that her father didn't care about her, and that her dad was more interested in performance than developing a relationship. Through the use of a systems approach, I was able to get the father to open up communications, and stop his negative approach.

A systems approach involves viewing family problems as a whole, rather than looking at each separate family member's difficulties in isolation. His daughter began to soften and connect more appropriately at home. Academic performance began to improve once this child felt affirmed by her father. Once she made the connection between her resentment toward her father and her academic performance, she was able to address her anger toward her father in more understandable and appropriate ways and reconnect with her dad. She took responsibility for her problem. She permitted that which was unconscious to be open to awareness. That is what is involved in stepping outside the bubble.

Children's Mentors

It's pretty clear that family of origin issues affects one's current behavior. Some of us were born into the wrong family. In such cases we need to create a new sense of family. Maybe when some of us were youngsters we had mentors along the way who acted as parental figures for us when we needed their support. Many of my patients talk about the mentors who affirmed them throughout their childhood. I remember when I was a child that I had a friend whose family would take me with them on a weeklong vacation to a camp in Michigan. To this day I can remember the excitement and anticipation of this summer event. Adults and children who really cared surrounded me. I still have special memories of the family who included me in their vacation plans to a weeklong retreat. I remember spending a great deal of time at this friend's house. On the weekends, his mother would provide us lunch before we set out to play. His parents were always supportive and encouraging in their communications with me.

My brother had a special adult friend. He was one those adults who was always upbeat. He always put a positive spin on things. He helped my brother get a job during the summers and provided immeasurable nurturance and advice. He was caring, compassionate, and a great life coach. My brother will never forget the impact that this man had on his life. His friend recently died of cancer, but my brother had an opportunity to talk with him days before he passed away. He was upbeat until his last breath. He provided my brother with support, guidance, and direction for his future. He showed my brother how to handle new tasks, helped him cope with his anger, and was an exceptional listener and coach.

The Effect of Childhood Patterns

Family-of-origin issues can and do affect current behavior. My clients typically gloss over or dismiss core issues of their history that impact current behavior. The most significant aspects of counseling are often mentioned within the last five minutes of a counseling session. It is not unusual for a client to mention a significant issue prior to leaving my office. When core issues are mentioned at the end of a session, they are often done in a nonchalant manner. When this pattern occurs, there is generally little emotion presented by the client, and the client appears to see no relationship between such casual remarks and the nature of their current problems.

Clients have a tendency to talk *about* their feelings rather than *feel* their feelings. This is like the difference between talking about walking and actually performing the task. Experiencing one's feelings and sharing them with others creates a sense of vulnerability. Many clients, particularly men, are hesitant to experience a sense of vulnerability. Many clients have been the victims of their parents underlying assumption that "children are to be seen, not heard." Children's needs to thwart their feelings are behind a myriad of emotional disorders. Learning to feel is like learning to ride a bicycle;

it takes time to master. I assist clients in cultivating feelings by probing sensitive issues, suggesting that they journal their feelings, requesting that they write about early childhood recollections, and writing letters to loved ones without delivering them.

Many children exhibit a pattern of projecting their pain. Instead of owning their feelings of shame, hurt, rejection, and anger they tend to make others responsible for what they are feeling. Unfortunately, those who are closest to those who project their emotions suffer the most. Those who we are most intimate with are the brave souls who put up with the projected baggage. With family, we feel safe enough to abuse them.

I used to see a teen whose father was highly intimidating. Often people who have fathers who are powerful and controlling tend to idealize the parent. In this case the teenager did just that. Her father could do no wrong. Meanwhile, she was projecting all the thwarted anger and rage toward her mother. It didn't matter what the father did, he was always right. It didn't matter what the mother did, she was always wrong.

One day, this girl went over the edge with her anger and rage and needed to be hospitalized. When she came out of in-patient treatment she met with me and an interesting shift had occurred. For the first time, the teen began experiencing negative feelings about her father. She expressed all the resentment she had felt for him. Following the individual session, we had a family session in which we focused on projected feelings. We discussed the safety net that the teen experienced in sharing her feelings with her mother. God forbid that she should ever challenge her father's opinions or style of parenting. He would have put her down in such a way that it would have been impossible to respond constructively. Healing began to occur when she realized that her rage toward her father was being directed toward her mother. She needed to find another way to manage her frustration and anger. I suggested journaling, using a punching bag, exercising, and meditation.

The Parenting Process

Parents many times deal with their kids the way they were disciplined. This may involve some archaic notions about parenting that no longer work in today's world with children. It is not unusual for adults to tend to believe that parenting primarily involves the use of power and control. In William Glasser's book, *The Identity Society*, he makes the point that the nature of parenting has changed over the last several decades.

Authority figures are no longer respected by virtue of the role they play. Teenagers are no longer compliant merely because their parents bark out orders. Glasser is very pragmatic about this issue. It's not a matter of what's right or wrong with reference to the values of parenting, it's what works. Typically, using control tactics no longer works with kids. Many teachers have a problem grasping this concept.

They believe they can coerce kids into doing schoolwork. It usually doesn't impact the child. Parents try to act authoritarian around their children and it backfires. Discipline is about role modeling respect, being firm, setting appropriate limits, and establishing consequences.

The most important step to discipline is creating a positive relationship with a child. Next, one must educate and coach kids on what you want them to do. Developing autonomy within your children involves coaching and educating them to take responsibility for themselves. Respect must be modeled for one's children, whether you like it or not. That's the way things are within our current cultural setting. You can complain about it, say it's not fair, but it's the reality. Life is a lot more fun when your children like you and respect you. Most children will do most anything for parents they respect. I realize that there are exceptions, and in those cases parents need not feel guilty for bad parenting. Some kids make poor choices regardless of how connected we are to them.

For parents, stepping out of the bubble may mean viewing the parenting process from a different perspective. It may mean giving up the image of parenting that was established during their childhood. Sometimes clients will internalize the image of parenting that was handed down to them even if that perception was intolerable. Sometimes caretaking of our kids involves doing the opposite of what was done to us. We need to get in touch with the kid within us. We need to remember what it was like to play and have fun. If our childhood wasn't fun, then we need to do some grief work and vow to make things different with our own children. If our inner parent is critical, we will most likely have unrealistic expectations for our children. We need to listen to the inner critic and let it speak. We may hear tones of the tyranny of the "shoulds." The inner critic or parent is full of moral injunctions. It is the judge and jury of our behavior. Combine that subpersonality with the pusher driver part of us and you have a toxic combination. The pusher driver is the inner part of us that says, "What you are doing is not good enough. You must always try harder." Parents need to get in touch with the inner critic and the pusher driver and identify with their contents and then detach. Parents will want to rationally respond to these subpersonalities with more reasonable ways of viewing specific issues. For example, the parent may want to respond with, "Ok, is it always necessary to do my best? Why can't I give myself permission to slack at times?" This process of rational responding will assist in clearing up the "muddy water" when it comes to coaching and advising our own children.

Children are not usually amenable to being lectured, being given moral injunctions, or being coerced into handling responsibilities. The critical issue with parenting is creating a sense of involvement. In this era, a parent must have established a positive relationship with a child before being able to promote understanding about what responsibilities that child must accomplish. A style of relating based on mutual respect, encouragement and coaching is essential. Parents need to listen to their children, and give them feedback with respect to different ways of viewing problems and issues.

Many times with my own children, I would use newspaper articles as teaching tools. For example, if some celebrity had died as a result of a drug overdose, I would hand them an article, ask them to read it and talk about their feelings regarding the situation. It is critical with children that as a parent you allow them to make value judgments about issues and problems. In a non-threatening manner, a parent can put a child in a position to make important value judgments. The key words are, "What would you do about this?" Or, "What do you plan on doing about this?" I call this "boxing the child in." When we, as parents, do the work of making value judgments for kids, they invariably dismiss our judgments. If we ask them what their plan is for handling a problem, we put the responsibility back on the children.

A number of years ago when I was working in the schools as a guidance counselor, I facilitated a parent-teacher conference for a passive teenager. During the conference, the teachers, one by one, were elaborating on the lack of motivation of this student. The student sat quietly at the conference while the parent feverishly took notes on missing assignments. This process continued until I finally interrupted. I responded to the parent, "Mrs. Jones, who's doing the work at this conference, you or your child?" She became rather embarrassed and got my point. I slid my clipboard down the conference table and requested that the child begin taking the notes on what was missing in his academic work.

Children need structure and parents need to provide it. It's amazing to me the number of parents who give their kids an allowance without demanding anything in return. I always suggest that parents set up a behavior chart providing their children with responsibilities. I have them put a monetary value on each daily item on the chart.

At first, I suggest that the chart be rather short. I have the parents and child focus on four or five areas that need improvement. Each night after dinner I suggest that the parents review the chart with the child. Areas accomplished successfully should be checked off on the chart or rewarded with tokens. At the end of the week, assuming the child has accomplished some tasks, he will get his allowance based on items completed. If the child saves his money, a ten percent monetary bonus may be given. If a child displays negative behavior such as prolonged temper tantrums, disrespect toward others and displays fits of anger, negative consequences are established. For negative consequences, focus on items that your child values the most and take them away for a reasonable amount of time. Negative consequences can be most effective as an immediate consequence for removal of privileges regarding serious behavioral infractions.

It is important as a parent that you are consistent in administering any behavioral consequence system. If you can't be consistent, then don't implement that system. It is also important that you use the behavioral consequence system as a way of removing yourself from power struggles with your kids. Parents make a major mistake in overexplaining themselves to their children. If you have a rule or consequence, it needs to be enforced, not justified.

Parents who justify their parenting weaken their role because they believe that their children will disapprove of them if they assert themselves. Approval has nothing to do with parenting. Children do not respect their parents if they do not set appropriate boundaries for their conduct. Providing behavioral structure for your children is a combination of building respect, establishing rules for behavior and developing responsibility in children.

As parents, we need to work on setting priorities with our children. We need to ask, "What are the important values that I want to stress and instill in my children?" Make sure that you major in the majors, not the minors. If you focus on minor behavioral infractions, there is a tendency to create conflict and power struggles with your children. In focusing on the behavioral minutiae, you and your child may lose sight of the significant values that you want to instill in your child. Your priorities for your child's character and responsibilities should be on tasks such as serving others, treating others with respect, doing volunteer work, making amends for mistakes, and contributing to the household by doing chores.

When I worked in the schools as a guidance counselor, I once had an exemplary student who needed a recommendation for college. I asked her to provide me with a worksheet or resume of her distinctions so that I could write a quality recommendation. In her worksheet, she told the story about how she would go to the landfill with her grandmother, look for broken dolls, take them home and repair them. Then she would deliver them to the children at a nearby orphanage. This is what I mean by encouraging children to cultivate worthwhile values and priorities.

As a parent, don't get overly caught up in fashion design, hair color, and types of music played by your children. Obviously, there are school dress codes and they need to be honored by your children. You may need to set household boundaries on the playing of loud music, but don't prohibit that outlet. Focusing on these issues can create unnecessary battles that go nowhere. If you continue to battle over less significant issues you create the conditions for bigger power struggles and resentment to emerge. Setting limits and holding children responsible is a delicate balance, but it's important to keep the lines of communications open with your children.

Parents need to communicate effectively their wishes and desires for their children. Children don't respond well to parents who holler, scream and reprimand in a scolding voice. In fact, as tempting as this behavior may be, you can bet that your child is tuning you out. You may also be creating an oppositional child through your well-intentioned, though ineffective means of parenting. Using positive reinforcement when your child gets things right, or using encouragement helps promote involvement. Maintaining consistent consequences, both positive and negative, are more effective than trying to coerce your child to do something for you.

Asking children to make value judgments about the choices they make is more effective than moralizing or pontificating about the right way to do things. If a child brings home a poor grade from school, resist the urge to lecture on the value of education. Ask your child, "Is what you're doing in this class good enough for you? How do you feel about this evaluation from the teacher? What steps can you take to improve your performance? What steps can you take to improve your behavior?"

Teach your child to take responsibility for his behavior. Do not accept excuses, such as "I hate this teacher, or I forgot to do some assignments." State your disappointment in what has happened and ask your child what he plans on doing to improve the matter. Box him in by making him accountable for coming up with a reasonable plan for improvement. Get it in writing if you wish, or with a handshake, but get a commitment for improved behavior. Never let your child off the hook. Make your child explain how he will change things for the better. Be calm, somewhat detached and persistent. Fostering involvement with your children which helps promote respect, setting character-building goals and priorities, and holding your children accountable for improved performance are essential characteristics of quality parenting.

The Identified Patient Syndrome

Sometimes in working with children I run into what I call the identified patient syndrome. The parents may bring a child to me with the underlying notion that fixing their child will stabilize the family. They want no responsibility in the counseling process for sharing information vital to the healing of the entire family system. I have has some parents drop their children off at the clinic door and pick them up afterward. This is not an acceptable treatment plan for me. In talking with the child, I sometimes get a picture that his problem is a metaphor for what is happening within the family. The child may be purposefully acting out as a way of drawing attention to family issues, or may be the victim of problems in the family outside the child's sphere of influence.

Typically, in such cases, the child may represent the most functional person in the family. Without hesitation I try to draw the parents into counseling, but they may be hesitant and attempt to focus attention back on their child as the source of the difficulty. So I work with the child and try the best I can to help them cope with a bad situation at home. I enjoy working with these children because they generally are insightful enough to have a solid grasp on issues at home that are perpetuating problems. What they need from me is a clearer understanding of how the home environment influences one's behavior and how I can help them to function within the dynamics at home.

The Art of Parenting

Parenting is an art. There are no manuals to give one the answers. Sometimes we learn through trial and error. The key for parents is refusing to do the same things repeatedly that don't work. If you are parenting in a way that is not getting results, try a different approach. Remember that mistakes are a necessary function of change. The goal of parenting is to help your children develop a sense of autonomy. Teaching them to be self-directed and responsible means that one must learn not to underfunction or overfunction as a parent. Underfunctioning or being an absent parent leaves a child feeling alone and without support. Many children have had absent fathers or mothers and this unfortunate pattern has left emotional scars. The lack of encouragement, nurturing, and affirmation has an impact on current behavior.

Many parents overfunction. They get overly involved in every aspect of their child's life. They may vicariously live their lives through their children. They speak for their children, think for their children, and act for their children. I always tell my parents, "Never do for a child what he can do for himself." Children learn to manipulate overfunctioning parents to get what they want. Since overfunctioning parents fear the disapproval of their children, they cater and give in to their wants and needs even if they are unreasonable requests. Fritz Perls, Gestalt therapist used to remark, "Kids need to be appropriately frustrated." What he meant was that overparenting creates an environment whereby children do not learn the skills necessary for self-regulation. Sometimes we need to let our kids figure things out without interference.

Teaching Children Civility

Have you ever had someone cut in front of you in line? How about letting the door slam on you when you are entering a restaurant? What about children screaming in a store because they want something they can't have? Or parents leaving their grocery cart in a parking lane rather than returning it to the cart return? These are obvious examples of incivility.

As parents, we focus a significant deal of attention with our children on school work and social activities. We spend far less time teaching, coaching, and encouraging our children to be sensitive, caring and concerned about the needs of others. We need to teach our children to be supportive of others, regardless of one's socio-economic status, behavioral idiosyncrasies or learning deficits. Many children feel the need to elevate themselves by taunting other kids who do not meet their social standards as friends. Hurtful bullying, teasing and gossiping may become a pattern for children who lack the skills of civility.

The most important skills we can teach our children are how to respect, value and support other children, especially those who are different from their lifestyle, cultural or religious background, social characteristics, or learning style. Our children need to learn from us to be inclusive in their social relationships, not exclusive.

Recently, I realized why the notion of civility was so important to me. One day when I was a teenager, my father invited me to attend work with him. I knew that he was a metallurgical engineer, but I had very little concept about the nature of his job. From my visit to my father's manufacturing plant, one memory still lingers about the trip. My father was a champion for the underdog. Although he was an executive manager, he walked through the plant and was known by all of the die-casting workers. It didn't matter who they were or what their role was, each worker would greet my father warmly and my dad would respond by acknowledging every person by name. My father's civility left a lifelong impression which I tired to role model and teach to my own children.

Years later, I remember how pleased I was with one of my patients, when a school psychologist conveyed to me a story about this young man's involvement with a special needs student. During my patient's high school career, he was a very popular student. The psychologist, who had complete a psycho-educational assessment on the special needs student, recalls how my client walked this student to different classes and befriended him. The special needs student played soccer with my client and they spent a great deal of time building a friendship. My patient's parents and I were proud that he had learned the lesson of civility in his relationships.

When children get off course in their road to civility, parents need to redirect them to be more kind, considerate and caring of all children. Specific civility concepts that parents can teach are:

- Teaching about multicultural tolerance and acceptance.
- Teaching children to care about others because it brings them meaning rather than expecting anything in return.
- Involving children in public service at a children's hospital.
- Teaching children to respect senior citizens by volunteering at independent living facilities.
- Teaching common courtesies, such as introducing oneself, shaking hands with others, and thanking people for doing kind gestures for them.
- Teaching children to share and play cooperatively with others.
- Teaching children to respect and assist those who are disabled or have learning limitations.
- Parents can demonstrate through word and action what civility means.

A friend of mine has a daughter who has just completed medical school. Getting into medical school was a highly competitive process. Although she had outstanding grades and very high entrance exam scores, the deciding factor in being accepted to medical school was not related to academics. She had served in the Peace Corp, and as any college recruiter will advise students, her global service in caring for people less fortunate was the deciding factor in her college admission.

Our world lacks a sense of civility. It is the responsibility of all of us in charge of children to make sure that the world of our children's future is more civil than the world we leave behind.

VIII. REFLECTIONS ON POP CULTURE

Much of the media culture is designed to create an illusion of experience, rather than depicting reality. Now you can vicariously live through someone else's experience in the comfort of your own home. You can find everything from desperate housewives, to television psychologists, to survival programs. It is now my understanding that one of our "fair and balanced" television networks has plans on airing a "reality show" that has the potential to trivialize the adoption process.

When we choose to live through other people's experiences, invariably we make a decision that our own reality is not good enough. We need to sensationalize living in order to make it tolerable. What an indictment of many people's lives. Are we so shallow that we need other people's experiences to give us a sense of meaning? Reality television is unreal. It is a caricature of reality. It is the bubble personified. It represents events and situations that are distortions of the truth.

People are hooked on the electronic media because it gives them a life, even if it is distorted or fictitious. People are afraid of coming out of the bubble because they must generate the courage to find their own life. To my amazement, as I was channel surfing last night there were at least three concurrent "survival" programs showing beautiful people being "counted out." What a distorted message to send our children. Some may say I'm being overly dramatic, but I don't think so. Let me take this media pop culture craze a step further.

Pop Culture and Teen Violence

A great deal of public attention has been focused on tragic shootings perpetrated in this country by youths. What other Western culture has the kind of homicidal teenage rage as ours? Journalists, political pundits and mental health providers all perceived the school shootings in different ways. Most of the explanations have left us feeling empty, not fully defining the nature of the problem.

I am not aware of many cultural prophets in this world, but one of them is an anthropologist from a community college in the Chicago suburbs. In 1994, I attended his presentation on the topic of "pop culture," and its impact on our society. Jesse Nash believes that the development of teen violence in our cultural fabric is not necessarily related to the typical psychological explanations such as poor self-esteem, defective parenting and dysfunctional families and emotional suffering. Instead he claims that our society has created a "cultural ethos" that promotes and perpetuates the intermingling of violence, sexuality, and animistic religion. Who is fostering this cultural paradigm shift? Entrepreneurs (such as movie/video makers, comic book distributors, and video game manufacturers), are out to make a lot of money at the expense of our kids.

If you have any doubts about the reality of this cultural shift, check out your local computer store or movie rental place for the top five movies rented to children. While you're at it, check on the latest video games that are available for your children. Children can systematically disable, shoot, and kill their opponent at the convenience of their own computer. They can heist cars like common criminals and play out the role of a terrorist as they perpetrate acts of violence. Children can even try their luck at shooting our former president, John F. Kennedy from the Dallas book depository! They can also replicate the bombing of the Oklahoma City Federal Building as they simulate the experience of Timothy McVeigh. Wayne Dwyer, noted author and speaker, recently indicated that most children, by the age of seven, have already absorbed up to fifteen hundred acts of murder on television. His point is, what does this tell us about the kind of emotional energy that our children are exposed to? How does this energy affect the behavior of our youth?

Dr. Nash conducted qualitative research in which he interviewed hundreds of teenagers who had habitually subjected themselves to pop culture media, including books, tapes, videos and video games. His conclusions are astonishing and frightening and concur with Dr. Dwyer's sentiments:

- Most of his subjects were unable to distinguish between fantasy and reality. They had lost touch with what is scientifically feasible and real.

- Most of the teens talked about violence with a sense of detachment, "What's the big deal?"

- Most of the students identified with the perpetrators of crime and violence as heroic, rather than identify with media images that portrayed positive energy and integrity.

- Most of the interviewees had taken hold of a value system that reflected images of sex, violence, and archaic religious symbolism.

- Most of the teens had a condescending attitude about adulthood and aging.

- Authority figures were mocked and devalued.

- Most of the teens were highly self-centered in their world-view.

These are the bubble kids. Playing out an image of reality, rather than living out real life experience. According to Nash, children are "hard-wired" developmentally in such a way that they are less capable of differentiating fantasy from reality than adults. Is it any wonder why some kids can walk into a school building, pull the alarm and proceed to shoot at their classmates and teachers like target practice? While these kids are in the bubble, they are playing out a scenario, a mythical game that they have observed with great regularity. There is no remorse in the bubble, because when one is in hiding he can't see reality through a clear set of lenses. Why do we wonder the reason that our youngsters are capable of such horrendous acts of violence? We have perpetuated this problem by allowing greedy entrepreneurs to prey on our most valuable resource, our children.

Our culture fosters an illusion of reality. It is pervasive throughout the fabric of our society. Several years ago, when I was touring Israel with my family, our tour guide commented, "The money-makers in America have ruined a whole generation of kids with their electronic gadgetry." Fortunately, many of our young people do not identify with these negative aspects of our electronic culture. They have more productive activities to hold their attention. The electronic media culture simulates a reality that often fosters acts of violence, aggression, and sexual behavior. Our pop culture teaches kids passive activity, and promotes a skewed perception of reality that values eternal youth, cosmetic beauty, the perpetration of violence, irresponsibility and a devaluation of adulthood.

About a year ago, I followed up with Jessie Nash by phone. I contacted him after a litany of school shootings appeared to confirm the hypothesis of his cultural research. Well-respected newspapers and magazines were reinforcing the validity of Dr. Nash's research, drawing a connection between pop culture and teen violence. For example, children who were trapped in Columbine High School during that tragedy had told the media that "it was surreal – it was as if a video game was being played out." I told Jessie how much I valued his work and asked him if he had done a series of presentations in light of the prophetic nature of his conclusions. His reply was, "No, I have not done many talks - I found that most people are not taking me seriously." "Why do you think that is?" I asked. Jessie went on to say, "I have found that the parents of the kids I am addressing are in cahoots with their children; the parents don't see a problem with many elements of pop culture; they don't want to see it." Unfortunately, his message was that many parents are accomplices to the downside of pop culture.

Have you been to a high school activity lately? Can you separate many of the mothers from the daughters in terms of the "baby doll clothes?" Have you seen the fathers at the video arcades playing out violent behaviors with their children? It's difficult to create awareness with the children because the parents have bought into the destructive aspects of pop culture media. Our dilemma is, "How do we refashion our culture in a way that does not cater to destructive images and behaviors that have been culturally accepted? How do we get our children and their parents to step out of the cultural bubble?"

Our Cosmetic Culture

Much of what we see in the media is cosmetic. Youth is personified and glorified. The use of steroid enhancing drugs to foster the "culture of youth" is widely role-modeled and promoted. Cosmetic surgery has become more of a necessity, rather than an option. I was doing some marketing for my business. I went to a plastic surgeon's office located within walking distance. As the office manager approached me, I believed that she had undergone plastic facial surgery. Why is it that I have a hunch that an individual has had plastic surgery? I am told it is not uncommon for administrative staffs that work in plastic surgeons' offices to have undergone facial reconstruction surgery. I guess they serve as a role model.

I told this office staff member who I was and responded with, "I am sure there are times when you have potential clients who have body misperception problems, who do not need surgery, and I am here to tell you that I can help them!" She looked at me with puzzlement. She was clueless as to what I was saying. I thanked her and was on my way. It appears that instead of new clothes, money, or other gifts, many teenage girls are now getting breast reconstruction surgery for their birthday.

Frequently, the media perpetuates this cosmetic image. Some friends of my wife and I have a son who is a correspondent in Afghanistan. He has indicated on numerous occasions that the "fair and balanced" news reporting that we receive from various news sources in the United States about the war is distorted. Many people are not interested in quality journalism. They want a spin on a story that will keep them awake. They want that story that will hold their attention through sensationalism.

Many people have an aversion to the truth about events. There are many Americans who still do not see the magnitude of the brutal treatment of prisoners during our current war. Many of us justify or minimize our government's mistakes. Many don't want to believe that there's a dark side to our institution of government. It's too painful to ask the question, "Could this brutality of detainees really be a systemic problem?" As I mentioned earlier, one of the ways of avoiding reality is to deify a person, situation, or institution.

How many flag draped coffins have we seen coming home from Iraq? How many stories of maimed or emotionally traumatized soldiers have been covered? People and institutions compartmentalize difficult and painful realities as a way of coping. Keeping things guarded protects the public from experiencing the full impact of events. By making a war appear cosmetic, people lose a sense of the magnitude of horrific events.

Our Fascination with Heroes

When people have no solid identity of their own, they become an extension of whoever or whatever they admire. Have you ever wondered why some people get caught up in the energy of famous individuals? There are many people who vicariously live out of the energy of heroes. Recently, after a game, a professional baseball pitcher was asked if he considered himself a role model for children. His response was, "Are you kidding, if you want a role model go home kids, go home and talk to your parents!" When John Lennon died, people who never knew him got so emotionally caught up at his vigil that they became hysterical. We seek out others who are heroic to define our own image. This pattern is doomed to leave us feeling empty, because no one from the outside can build our inner sense of self.

IX. REFLECTIONS ON THE GROWTH ZONE

There are many people who would rather stay in hiding than come out and play. These are the people who prefer to feel victimized by life. "If only" is their motto. "If only things were different." Things are never *different* from the way they are, they are always *just* the way they are. Unfortunately, reality cannot be manipulated to make it fit the way the victim wants it. Life is a continual process of grieving and letting go of losses. As we age, one must give up the illusion of adolescence, physical prowess, personal beauty, physical energy, a changing world, unmet dreams, and the temporal nature of life. But on the other side of our grief and loss are hope, love, companionship, lasting memories and playfulness. We really can recreate ourselves. We don't have to live in the "rear view mirror." We can't go back to the way things were anyway. It's over.

The Persistence of Moving On

Stepping out of the bubble means moving on, no matter what the circumstances. It means being a fighter, the kind of fighter that never gives up hope. We can envision in our minds what we want the future to hold. Then we must go out into the world and work to make it happen. Complete failure is not an option. Mistakes *are* an option. Learning from our mistakes and moving forward is productive. We need to understand that the world isn't going to change to accommodate our self-pity. Anything we get, we must pursue with diligence. This is what persistence is about. It is a wonderful character trait. Persistent people are continuously knocking on the door of change. They want things to be better for themselves and others. They refuse to give in to problems and difficulties that surround them. Persistence is the quality that keeps you going when you don't feel like trying anymore. You refuse to let obstacles stand in the way of successful living.

Successful Living

Many define successful living as having the right car, living in the right neighborhood, and having the right job. Success for many is defined by the amount of money one makes. Many of my clients have had all of these things and have watched them fade away in a moments notice. What sustains you when the American dream is no longer a reality? When you are no longer around, will you be known for your professional talent? How about your ability to make a lot of money? How about the way you look? We must think about the character traits we want to leave as our legacy.

Being a fully functioning individual is about being true to whom you are and letting things be the way they are. Many of us spend an inordinate amount of time trying to change our lives and reality to fit a preconceived notion that we have about life. We try to manipulate life as a way of functioning, avoiding any anguish that accompanies living in current awareness. By living in the rear view mirror, we cheat ourselves out of all that life has for us in the present and future. Live in the moment, let go of the past, and don't try to anticipate the future. Move into the future with the conviction that all will work out. Your convictions will bring positive energy into the future and will help you realize your dreams. Believe that everything is possible. Nothing is out of your range of success. Your perception of events determines the kind of thinking that you will create. Reframe negative thoughts and circumstances so that things will move in a positive direction for you.

Getting Life in Perspective

Several years ago I went for my usual hairstyle appointment. When I got there I realized that my hairstylist had double-booked my appointment. She was very late in getting to me and then she had me wait while she finished up with her other customer. I was seething. My train of thought was, "I pay this woman well. I always tip her generously, how could she do this to me?" I started thinking that she was greedy and selfish. Finally, after her other customer had left, I confronted her about my concern. She indicated that her mother had suffered a stroke and that she needed to leave town on an emergency basis to visit her. She was sorry for the need to crunch her schedule. Needless to say, I felt like a louse. Here I was, agitating about a haircut, while this woman was frightened for her mother and couldn't wait to get to her hospital room. Life is all about the way we frame things. It is about getting issues in perspective. If we attempt to see events and circumstances in a positive light, we will feel lighter and will cope with stress more effectively.

Many of us get caught up in the small stuff. Richard Carlson has written several books that deal with the issue of examining our perception of events. Most of the issues in life that we agitate about are not worth the energy. At my office, I was having trouble parking in our behavioral health office area. Since it is a new complex and work was continuing on other buildings, two flatbed trucks were blocking my ability to find a parking spot. I finally parked in an undercover area reserved for one of our practice administrators. The secretarial staff encouraged me to move my car as soon as possible because the assigned person was infuriated. I immediately left my office and noticed that the flatbed trucks had left and I moved my car. At the end of the day she confronted me over the parking issue. She was incensed. I mentioned how I had just received a phone call from my prior practice. One of my former colleagues had gone in for a physical and they had found a cancerous tumor. When I mentioned this story to her, she failed to understand my point. My point….life is too short to major in the minors.

Healing the Dark Side

What stays in the bubble and is avoided will ultimately rear its ugly head and make itself known to the world. We cannot deny the darkness of our history. Without the healing of the darkness within, it will reemerge as a weapon of destruction in our personal and professional life.

There is a time in everyone's life when a choice must be made. Will I carry on the legacy of the past by avoiding the wounds associated with my history, or will I courageously face the pain of my history and reexamine it? If we can reexamine our past, we can then move forward in a new direction. We can recreate ourselves and make our life more meaningful. The mystery is, why do some choose to step out of the bubble while others do not? The truth is that many who do choose the path of courageous living recognize that we are ultimately responsible for our own direction and feel an urgency to change.

However, it is very easy to give up trying to improve our condition. It is so easy to avoid reality. Since many of us are rather lazy, it becomes our way of coping with reality. It becomes comfortable to remain emotionally stagnant. But, if we play out the martyr role, we may falsely cling to the notion that others will solve our problems for us. Many of us, on some level, believe that someone or something is magically going to rescue us from our problems. We keep waiting and hoping that this will happen as our lives run their course.

Giving oneself permission is the way to find the passage toward adulthood. Recognizing that there is no one to rescue us but ourselves is the key. On some level, most of us hold onto the illusion that our parents, whether dead or alive, will bail us out of our unhappiness. As Mildred Newman and Bernard Berkowitz profoundly proclaim in their book, *How to Be Your Own Best Friend,* we must emotionally let go of our parents. We must let them go and transcend them in how we conduct our lives. As psychotherapist author Sheldon B. Kopp says, we must be an "on-your-own, take-care-of-yourself-cause-there-is-no-one-else-to-do-it-for-you-grownup." No one is going to come and rescue us. The permission lies within.

Giving oneself permission is the difference between living in a bubble and stepping out. We all have needs, wants, and aspirations. Sometimes these desires get put on hold because we are afraid of failure or afraid of what others might think. Many of us feel underutilized. We feel guilty for not realizing our potential. Appropriate guilt, the recognition that we have fallen short of our goals, is necessary if we are to change and grow. We have to be upset enough at our situation in order to change it. Many times people will say, "I'm sick of the way I behave, I've had it!" I remind them that they must get very tired of it before they will be willing to change the behavior. As reformed alcoholics sometimes say, "sometimes you've got to hit rock bottom."

The Urgency of Life

Life is too short. But the fear of passing time may give us an urgency about making things right. Such a feeling of urgency may create the conditions for changing the quality of our character and behavior. We don't have forever to redeem what remains lost. We must make amends with those we have offended, heal our relationships with those we care about, and move on. This is what fully functioning people do. They don't wait, they don't procrastinate, but they act. It was Roberto Assagioli, the great Italian physician and psychiatrist who wrote the book, *The Act of the Will.* The entire book is based on the assumption that people can learn to mobilize, to act.

When I worked in education as a guidance counselor, I would invariably meet with a child who would respond to a request that I had made by saying, "I'll try to do it!" To demonstrate to the student the impact of trying, I would say to him, "Try to get out of the chair you are sitting in." The child would look at me dumbfounded, and I can assure you that in thirty years of working with children not one ever stood up following my request. Next I would say, "Get up out of that chair!" No problem, every student would stand up immediately. Trying is another word for excuse making. People don't try to change; they commit themselves to doing it. It is only when one gives up the illusion of trying and makes a serious effort to alter one's behavior that real change emerges.

The Paradigm Shift

Changing one's lifestyle calls for a paradigm shift. Many of you may remember William Deming. William Deming had a theory of management (lead management) and went to the big three U.S. automakers with a plan for changing their manner of doing business. Rather than maintain a hierarchal system of management, he developed a system that gave workers a vested interest in what they were producing. His theory of management called for collaboration, team-building, managerial coaching by example, and positive encouragement and reinforcement of employees. He felt that a shift in the management style would give the American automakers a needed edge in dealing with foreign competition from Europe and Japan. The CEO's of the American automakers couldn't catch a vision of his management style. They refused to listen.

With that in mind, he took his theory to the competitors. Our automotive competitors from Japan utilized Mr. Deming's collaborative management style and began producing automobiles that were significantly superior in quality to American counterparts. Because the workers were granted a vested interest in corporate goals and were positively reinforced for their efforts, the workers were motivated to produce a quality product. When workers are coerced to perform through a hierarchal management scheme, employees tend to do just enough to meet minimum standards. Excellence in quality fails, because the workers feel alienated from management and an adversarial relationship develops. Resentment breeds, and workers meet the minimum standards necessary to get their paycheck.

Motivational Theory

People's needs for validation, support, loyalty, and reinforcement must be met in order for motivation to increase. Lecturing, moralizing, dictating, coercing and being punitive do not work. And yet many parents, teachers, and managers continue to operate on a system of principles that are of no value. It's a form of tunnel vision that is self-defeating. The theory of bossing people to get a desired result is archaic and self-defeating. Most people boss-manage because they don't know any better, or because they are insecure about their competency. Managers who are insecure about their job abilities tend to overcompensate by trying to prove to others how ruthless they can be in the pursuit of performance. A quality manger can admit mistakes, role model appropriate professional behavior for employees, and connect with those he oversees.

Those who step out of the bubble are "paradigm shifters." They seek information, knowledge, and truth wherever it may be found. They are not afraid to look within every corner to find new ways of accomplishing tasks. They are creative and energized. They feel fulfilled in their personal and professional endeavors. They look forward to new and risky challenges. They are great listeners. In fact, they listen more than they talk. Vulnerability is not a sign of weakness, but represents an opening to new ways of thinking and feeling. These people will take responsibility for their mistakes.

Redeeming the Intergenerational Trap

Dysfunctional patterns of behavior may follow an intergenerational system of relating. That which is not brought to awareness in one generation follows the next. Many women, who experience domestic abuse as a child, maintain the same pattern in the relationships they establish within adulthood. Since they have no foundation for what a healthy relationship looks like, they believe that dysfunction and abuse is a normal part of relationships. They learn to "settle" because they have no frame of reference for what would be considered a healthy relationship. Many times, they bounce from one relationship to the next, looking for the love that they never received during childhood.

The cycle can only be broken when the person finally realizes that she has been duped. She recognizes that horrible nightmare that has followed her from childhood to partner after partner. She must learn to grieve and mourn the past and move on in a new direction. The paradigm shift includes a new way of looking at the nature of relationships and their value. Settling for dysfunction is no longer acceptable. Setting the bar much higher and believing that one deserves to be treated with respect is necessary. Only then will the nightmare of the past be broken. We all need role models in our lives that exemplify the characteristics of respect, integrity, compassion, empathy and courage.

People who live in a bubble always have lowered expectations. When it comes to protecting and nurturing themselves they fail to see their own blind spots. They will remain in abusive relationships with no regard to their own needs. These clients appear oblivious to how demeaned and poorly treated they are by their partners. They have never been taught that they are worth more than what they are experiencing. Who along the path of their life has taught them that they deserve better? Who has taught them that they have the inner strength to create a better life for themselves? Who has taught them to display the kind of courage needed to let go of a failing relationship? As a therapist, it is my role to admonish and act as a therapeutic model to strengthen, empower, and assist my client to understand her worth.

Redeeming the Past

We don't need to live in the cloud of our past any longer. We can redeem the past and move on to develop a new future. A client of mine who has recently been struggling with the issue of giving herself permission to change directions, provides a clear example. She is afraid to succeed because her parents personified failure. She feels guilty for leaving them behind in her emotional quest to find psychological growth and healing. We must all emotionally let go of our parents if we are to create our own destiny. This means that we must not be afraid of doing better than our parents did. It's really acceptable to move beyond their level of success and well-being.

This client had an interesting dream. In the dream she was on a roller coaster enjoying the freedom of the ride when all of a sudden the person in the car in front of her was cut in half. All that showed was the abdomen of an unrecognized person. She woke up terrified. She wanted an explanation.

Since I believe that aspects of a dream can represent specific features of a person's life, I had a hunch. I hypothesized that she was on a journey toward wholeness and that she felt cut off from realizing her dreams due to internal conflict over permission to succeed. I asked her if my interpretation fit. She was quite amazed to see the parallels in her own life. I believe that dreams and synchronistic experiences happen for a reason. As M. Scott Peck claims, they are "gifts of grace." These experiences come into our lives because we are open to new insights. They represent powerful tools for change. My client's dream was symbolic of all that was happening in her current experience. These "happenings" are tools that assist us in the pursuit of spiritual and psychological growth and development. For my client, it was a potent message to assist her in her journey toward fulfillment and growth.

The Power of Words

Don Ruiz, in his book called the *Four Agreements*, talks about the power of words. Most of us have had things said about us that were emotionally damaging. Early childhood recollections of slights and criticism appear to impact all of us in negative ways. We tend to vividly remember comments that were expressed in a way that made us feel small. I can still remember how small I felt when a girl I dated to the homecoming dance turned on me the following week by giggling and laughing about me in front of her friends. I felt devastated. I couldn't understand how a night I enjoyed turned out to be such a humiliating experience because of the words and body language of a young girl. I never wanted to date again. Negative early recollections have a way of crystallizing and emerging as "hot buttons" later on in life.

I had a client who had a first grade teacher who was intimidating and mean. He is a very sensitive guy, and the mere mention of that experience still causes an emotional reaction. In fact, it was a presenting issue that we dealt with within the first several sessions. When a partner in a relationship continues to get beaten down through the use of negative communication, those words ultimately create a sense of indifference. After a period of time, the partner quits caring. They shut down to the power of words and give up on the relationship. The Bible says that "love covers a multitude of sins" but some words and actions are so damaging that irreparable harm may be done. Forgiveness no longer has much meaning. Trust has been broken.

Healing is like pealing an onion. It's one layer at a time. Unfortunately, many of us keep finding new layers! My experiences, those of my friends and clients, emerged as a catalyst for writing this book. I do not want others to feel numb, to feel small, and feel the persistent pain that comes from those who have created disappointment. I no longer want others to avoid, to hide in the bubble, and to find ways of circumventing the process of "moving through their pain" toward psychological growth. I want everyone to come out and join the party, to get in the game and share their life with others. God bless those, like my wife, who have helped me to grow and change. I wish positive health and growth for all of my friends, family and patients, and for all of you who take the time to read this book. Step out of the bubble, it's worth it.

MY THERAPEUTIC LAUNDRY LIST OF TRUTHS

1. What is, is whether you like it or not.

2. Courage is moving forward in spite of utter terror.

3. You can run, but you cannot hide (for long).

4. There is nothing admirable about avoiding hurt.

5. Hurt is the inevitable byproduct of significant decisions we make.

6. Quit holding on to the burden of other's feelings.

7. Give yourself permission to be a grown-up.

8. Give up the approval/disapproval trap.

9. Your voice must be more convincing than all the other clamoring voices.

10. You are enough.

11. Belief and faith are opposites.

12. Feel the full impact of the way things are and were.

13. If you go into the wilderness, you will come out.

REFERENCES

Assagioli, R. (1973). The act of the will. Penguin: New York.

Assagioli, R. (1976). Psychosynthesis. Penguin Books: New York.

Beck, A.T. (1976). Cognitive therapy and the emotional disorders. New York: International University press.

Berkowitz, B. and Newman, M. (1974). How to be your own best friend. Ballantine Books: New York.

Carlson, R. (1997). Don't sweat the small stuff...and its all small stuff. Hyperion Press: New York.

Cummings, T.W. (1980). Help for the fearful flyer. Freedom From Fear of Flying, Inc.: Coral Gables, Florida.

Dwyer, W. (2004). The power of intention. Hay House, Inc.: Carlsbad, CA.

Ellis, A. (1962). Reason and emotion in psychotherapy. Lyle Street: New York.

Fowler, J.W. (1995). Stages of faith: the psychology of human development and the quest for meaning. Harper Collins Publishers: New York.

Glasser, W. (1965). Reality therapy. Harper Row: New York.

Glasser, W. (1998). Choice theory: A new psychology of personal freedom. Harper Collins Publishing, Inc.: New York.

Gunn, W.H. (1987). The joy of flying: Overcoming the fear. Wings Publications: Mission, Kansas.

Hanh, T.N. (1976). The miracle of mindfulness. Beacon Press: Boston

Horney, K. (1987). Final lectures. W.W. Norton and Company: New York.

Kopp, S.B. (1972). If you meet the buddah on the road kill him. Bantam Books: New York.

Kushner, H.S. (1981). When bad things happen to good people. Avon Books, Inc.: New York.

Nash, Jessie, W. (1994). Neotribalism: Postmodern pop culture and marvel comics. Annual meeting of the popular culture association. Chicago, April 6, 1994.

Peck, M. S. (1978). The road less traveled. Simon and Schuster: New York.

Peck, M. S. (1987). The different drum. Simon and Schuster: New York.

Perls, F. (1973). The gestalt approach and eye witness to therapy. Science and Behavior Books: New York.

Powell, J. (1996). Why am I afraid to tell you who I am? Thomas More Publishing: Allen, Texas.

Puhakka, K. & Hanna, F.J. (1988). Opening the POD: A therapeutic application of Husserl's phenomenology. Psychotherapy, 25-4.

Rogers, C.R. (1965). Client-centered therapy. Houghton Mifflin Co.: Boston.

Rowan, J. (1990). Subpersonalities: the people inside us. Routledge: London.

Ruiz, D. M. (2000). The four agreements. Amber-Allen Publishing: San Rafael, California.

Schwartz, J.M. (1996) Brain Lock. Regan Books: New York.

Stone, H. and Winkleman, S. (1989). Embracing Ourselves: The voice dialogue manual. New World Library: California.

Watts, A. W. (1951). The wisdom of insecurity. Pantheon Books: New York.

Whitfield, C. L. (1987). Healing the child within. Health communications, Inc.: Deerfield Beach, Florida.

Young, J. E. (1990). Cognitive therapy for personality disorders: a schema-focused approach. Professional Resource Exchange: Sarasota, Florida.

Printed in the United States
95423LV00003B/302/A